76/5

Mind Shift

Also by Lourens Schlebusch

Books

Conduct Disorders in Youth
The Vulnerable: Understanding and Preventing Suicide (Editor)
Mind-Body Synthesis: The Interactive Health Care Equation
Clinical Health Psychology: A Behavioural Medicine Perspective
(Editor)
A Basic Guide to the Diagnosis and Treatment of Depression (Editor)
Suicidal Behaviour (Editor)
Suicidal Behaviour 2 (Editor)
Suicidal Behaviour 3 (Editor)
Cancer Can Be Beaten: A Biopsychosocial Approach (Editor)
Proverbial Stress Busters
South Africa Beyond Transition: Psychological Well-being (Editor)
Psychological Recovery from Cancer

Video/Audiotapes

Stress Management (Video)
Living With Cancer (Audio Tape)
Maintenance of Self: A Practical Guide to Stress Management (Video)
Maintenance of Self: A Practical Guide to Stress Management (Audio
Tape)
Stress Management: A Practical Guide (Audio Tape)
Stress Management: A Practical Guide for the Health Care Professional
(Audio Tape)

Mind Shift

Stress Management
and your Health

by

Lourens Schlebusch

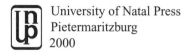 University of Natal Press
Pietermaritzburg
2000

Published by University of Natal Press
Private Bag X01, Scottsville 3209, South Africa

ISBN 0 86980 956 3

Cover design by Brett Armstrong
Inside illustrations by Olive Anderson

Typeset by Alpha Typesetters cc, New Germany, South Africa
Printed and bound by Kohler Carton and Print
PO Box 955, Pinetown 3600, South Africa

Contents

Part Two
How stress affects you

Part Three

What can you do about it?

CHAPTER 7

CHAPTER 8

CHAPTER 9

Acknowledgements

I ACKNOWLEDGE the co-operation and support of my various colleagues and friends. Thanks are also due to those colleagues who reviewed the content of the manuscript and for their many helpful suggestions in this regard. The invaluable secretarial and word processing help from my secretary, Erna van der Walt, is much appreciated. I would also like to thank my literary agent, Isabel Cooke, for her expertise and guidance, my editor, Sally Hines, for her proofreading and other indispensable assistance, and Karen Loly and Karen Mac Gregor for their valuable contribution.

I welcome correspondence and constructive suggestions from readers. Please write to: Professor Lourens Schlebusch, Department of Medically Applied Psychology, Faculty of Medicine, University of Natal, Durban, Private Bag 7, Congella 4013, South Africa.

Preface

THE basic, paradoxical message in this book is that stress can be extremely harmful to your health, yet not all stress is bad for you. Intrinsic to this is your perception of stress and how to change that perception in order to make sense of the paradox of stress and cope better with negative stress. By applying the techniques in this book you can learn to become the master instead of the victim of stress. In pursuing this approach, I hope to set in motion a process that will also assist you, on the one hand, to modify those aspects of your lifestyle that contribute to unhealthy stress and ill-health and, on the other hand, to acquire and promote those that will enhance your well-being and quality of life so that you can be better equipped to deal with future stress. This means accomplishing psychological self-empowerment by achieving control and by putting yourself into the psychological driver's seat.

With knowledge, training, practice and experience you can succeed and live a healthier life. It's your choice. Most stress research is based on investigating three common types of response to stress – that is, the physiological, psychological and behavioural responses in which the body and mind interact closely with each other. This book provides basic knowledge about these and other areas of stress which are considered fundamental to effective stress management, yet it is not a substitute for professional psychological help and I would advise against using it as such. Because stress can be associated with various medical or psychological disorders, I advise that you consult an appropriate health care professional to establish whether you require professional help. This would also apply if you suffer from severe stress that you cannot cope with on your own.

The content of this book is based partly on other as well as on my own research into stress and the mind–body connection, and partly on experience gained through many years of teaching stress management to health care students and professionals and presenting numerous workshops to a variety of health care, corporate and educational organisations. To some extent, then, I take an integrative approach to stress management in this book, which contains most of what I teach in therapy, lectures and workshops. The contents also incorporate some ideas from my two previous books on stress: *Proverbial Stress Busters* and *Psychological Recovery from Cancer*. You would find it useful to read these books as background to this one as they augment each other.

You may ask, 'Why another book on stress?' The answer is simple. Despite the many publications on this subject, stress remains one of the major influences in our lives and people can learn to manage their stress. Furthermore, stress means different things to different people and each person experiences stress uniquely. Broad, basic guidelines provided in an easily understood manner and adaptable to the individual are therefore necessary to manage stress.

In addition, several other reasons motivated me to write this book. My interest in stress management originally derived from extensive work with patients with potentially life-threatening diseases or conditions and their families, who needed help to cope with the resultant stress. A distinct need for a practical guide became apparent during my clinical work with them and with the many other individuals who have struggled to cope with the stress in their lives and its inevitable ramifications. Such treatment was usually in either individual or small group therapy sessions. Often during these sessions, when I listened to my patients' needs, I realised that I had little to offer in such limited time. They needed guidelines to help themselves and apply elsewhere and to other situations, because dealing with stress can be a complex process and in today's pressurised life more often than not it becomes a lifelong task. Because there will always be stress, there is no one-off quick and easy fix that suits everybody or that will suffice for all future potential stress. Accepting this, my patients themselves often expressed the need for a guide they could acquire and refer to when needed – even long after therapy had ended.

Also, the cost of stress is enormous, and I thought there must be some way to reduce this. Not only do we have to consider the overt, obvious costs related to a reduced quality of life and physical and psychological disorders, but also the price society has to pay for the hidden costs. These lurk behind stress-related accidents, absenteeism, diminished productivity, broken relationships, substance abuse and a host of other problems that reflect people's psychological anguish resulting from the inability to cope with stress. Although it is not easy to place a monetary value on health care, this is regularly being attempted by economic analyses of health care costs in efforts to find methods to curb ever-spiraling costs. I believe that one way is to educate larger numbers of people about the effects of stress, in order to teach them to accept responsibility for maintaining their own health and to prevent stress-related ill health.

Finally, there are many stressed people who do not have the time or the resources to attend therapy sessions or stress management seminars or workshops, but who would like access to the issues discussed there. This is particularly relevant for developing communities. This book has also been written to fill part of that vacuum.

There are many different methods to deal with stress and to release the build up of tension in your mind and body. The approach to stress management described in this book is based on mastering 15 of the most powerful stress stoppers. Each chapter takes you through a summary of the principles underlying one of these stress stoppers, and represents a synthesis of the results of much research and practical experience. The first 6 stress stoppers (Parts One and Two) involve identifying and understanding stress and the effects of stress on you. The purpose is that this knowledge should put you in a position to do a personalised evaluation of your stress in order to cope with it. This is important because you need to know what happens to you under stress, what you need to change and you need immediate feedback to motivate you to take action. Part Three discusses the other 9 stress stoppers which allow you to take practical action to reduce your unhealthy stress.

Foreword

STRESS has been a historically known phenomenon, and has increasingly become a widely used term in daily communication. With the vast amount of research in the clinical and behavioural sciences that has proliferated in this area, our understanding of stress has correspondingly grown, and is now universally accepted as having a profound effect on all facets of our existence. A mild degree of stress, like anxiety, may be therapeutic with respect to helping fortify one's psychological immune system. However, living in a time warp, which is characterised by a rapidly changing society in its energetic quest for improving and preserving life has, somewhat paradoxically, been generating a new genre of stress-related diseases, which may not necessarily be physical in nature, but may also influence all aspects of thinking, emotions and behaviour. Stress may, quite appropriately, be termed a 'Millennium Malady', and is something that all individuals need to be aware of, and more important, to be equipped with the necessary psychological medicinal skills to cope with stress in the new millennium.

Professor Lourens Schlebusch has developed an excellent reputation as an academic, researcher and clinician. He has published extensively, and is much sought-after for the valuable contributions he has made both in the clinical field, as well as towards the professionalisation of psychology as a rapidly growing and ever-popular discipline. This book serves as a wonderful example of some of his fine work. Designed to appeal to a wide spectrum of people, and written in a user-friendly style, it should be an integral part of an individual's personal study collection, as well as a resource text in academic libraries. It may be used as a life- and work-skills study book, or as a reference text for research and teaching, and by professionals and the public alike. In conclusion, in a strange way, this book beautifully captures the concept of stress and even a simple reading of it may be therapeutic with respect to enhancing our understanding of this enigmatic term called 'Stress'.

Dr Ahmed S. Vanker

Consultant Clinical Psychologist
Child and Adolescent Mental Health Service
Leicestershire & Rutland Healthcare – NHS Trust
Department of Clinical Psychology, Faculty of Medicine
University of Leicester
Leicester UK

Part One

What is stress?

Knowledge and awareness are the first steps in coping with stress. Before looking at ways to reduce the stress in your life you must have a clear idea of what stress is and how much stress you suffer from.

CHAPTER 1

It's not what you do, it's the way you do it

STRESS IS NOT NEW

STRESS is not new. It has always existed. People are a troubled species, and stress has become a major problem as we enter the new millennium. The difficulties of yesteryear have given way to those of a different sort today, punctuated on the one hand by a sense of change and urgency with so much to do and cope with in so little time, and on the other hand by perceptions of emptiness, uncertainty and meaninglessness, with stress gnawing away at the very core of our being. Anybody can become a victim of the ravages of stress. Scientific studies conclude that nobody escapes stress entirely and sooner or later the young or old, rich or poor fall prey to it, although some lifestyles invite it more than others. It doesn't help to try and wish it away.

What does help, however, is to know what it is, identify the stressors and their causes in your life and how they affect you, and then learn coping skills to deal with them. Knowledge of stress is one of the most powerful tools you can have, along with adequate stress management skills. These sound like obvious observations, yet they reflect significant scientific truths, because so many people are constantly seeking a better understanding of stress and how to cope with it. Perhaps this is also true because the term stress is so frequently heard, but seldom adequately explained for all to understand.

STRESS AS A FORCE

Although the word 'stress' has been used to describe human behaviour for a long time, the concept has only recently been more refined in psychological circles. Contributions from the sciences of physics and engineering have assisted in developing a better grasp of stress and its current use in psychology. Stress originally really means a force. Three terms are used to define this force from this original perspective: stress, strain and load. These concepts have been useful in understanding stress from a psychological perspective.

So, let's translate the lessons taken from physics and engineering into psychological terms. Take the example of a car. If you should apply continuous force to any of its inanimate components, eventually what will happen is stress will ensue and it will take strain. Let's say you have difficulty in turning the ignition key when you want to start the engine and the steering lock of the car is engaged. You decide that you have to use some force, but it still won't turn. If you continue to apply the force and the stress becomes worse, the key starts to take strain which causes molecular changes inside it. If it still won't turn and you continue to apply force, the key might bend and perhaps eventually even break. The reaction to the stress comes from outside as well as from within. Similarly, in human beings a life event or daily hassle can end up in stress. If this stress continues to be applied to your life, you could end up with symptoms such as anxiety and others. If these symptoms are not dealt with, they can lead to discomfort or even disorders, mental or physical. This is illustrated in Table 1.1.

TABLE 1.1

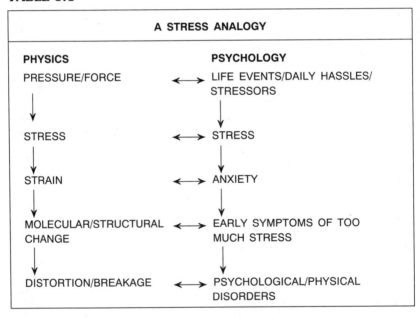

A STRESS ANALOGY	
PHYSICS	**PSYCHOLOGY**
PRESSURE/FORCE ⟷	LIFE EVENTS/DAILY HASSLES/ STRESSORS
↓	↓
STRESS ⟷	STRESS
↓	↓
STRAIN ⟷	ANXIETY
↓	↓
MOLECULAR/STRUCTURAL CHANGE ⟷	EARLY SYMPTOMS OF TOO MUCH STRESS
↓	↓
DISTORTION/BREAKAGE ⟷	PSYCHOLOGICAL/PHYSICAL DISORDERS

A DEFINITION OF STRESS AND STRESSORS

Stress can be understood as the result of an interaction between you and your environment. Nothing is stressful unless you interpret it as such. In this sense, stress is a relationship between you and your environment when you perceive and evaluate your environment as a threat to your well-being. You do this when the environmental demands exceed your coping resources. Put differently, stress is your physiological, psychological and behavioural reactions when you attempt to adapt and adjust to internal and/or external demands or pressures that you cannot cope with. From a psychological point of view, stress can be any action or situation that places special physical or psychological demands on you that upset your equilibrium. Perception, along with evaluation or appraisal, assumes central position in this process. Three types of appraisal can be distinguished: primary appraisal occurs when you evaluate the importance of the situation (stressor) for your well-being; secondary appraisal occurs when you feel you can do something about it; and re-appraisal occurs when there are changes in your evaluation as a result of changes in the situation.

Stress, then, is brought on by a stressor. A stressor can be any event, situation, person or object that you perceive as stressful and that you have difficulty in coping with and that can, therefore, result in negative stress. Obviously such stressors can vary widely, and the causes of stress are many. Although different people may respond differently to them, a sure fact of life is that stressors form part of everyone's existence. It must be remembered that past experiences, anticipation and imagination can also be powerful stressors. For example, you might complain of anxiety when you perceive a future event to be stressful (anticipatory anxiety). Anticipation of a future event and its consequences can elicit stress. Or you might worry about a past event (especially something you can now do little about) that makes you feel stressed, or about something that doesn't matter or that cannot be changed. This futile, needless worrying causes you stress because it makes you carry emotional baggage. Usually when you perceive a situation as controllable, it forms an important part of your sense of competence and coping. When you see the situation as uncontrollable, it contributes to stress because you feel you cannot cope. Certainty and uncertainty also play a role here. If you have a high degree of certainty of the positive outcome of an event, your hope is transformed into confidence and less stress. The opposite is also true. Uncertainty of a positive outcome will produce more stress. When this happens, your coping skills need to be sharpened. The way you deal with stress is referred to as coping. Coping itself involves both active and adaptive processes. It is the constantly changing efforts you employ to manage demands made on you. Coping can be problem-focused or emotion-focused.

Problem-focused coping strategies are your attempts to control a stressful situation, locating its causes and then changing or removing them. These are attempts at primary control whereby you adjust the situation to help you cope with stress. Emotion-focused coping strategies are your actions which serve to diminish negative emotions. These are attempts at secondary control to reduce the increased arousal caused by the stress and to regulate your emotions caused by the stress – that is, in a way you now adjust to the situation causing the stress, especially when your primary control efforts (problem-focused coping) fail. If, on top of this, you experience a restriction of freedom of action to do what you have to in order to cope, it could lead to all sorts of negative emotions like anger, frustration and loneliness. The results can further increase your stress. It is, therefore, essential to empower yourself psychologically to avoid being sucked up into such a negative vortex. There are many successful ways of coping, and a variety of techniques are discussed in this book, but in essence coping involves a positive and constructive way of solving problems and letting go of that unnecessary emotional baggage that results in stress.

Stress has a lot to do with the way your body and mind adapt to the demands made by change, which in turn has to do with your perception of those demands and change. Perception is a psychological function that enables you to receive, process and interpret information about your environment. This assumes great meaning as part of the process of interpreting events that affect the psychological control you should strive for. How perception relates to thoughts, feelings and your ability to cope with stress is discussed more fully in Chapter 7.

CHRONIC AND ACUTE STRESS

Sometimes stress can be chronic or enduring, such as in a person who suffers for years in an unrewarding personal or work relationship. At other times stress can be acute (sudden and intense) which can lead to a crisis, such as in a sudden traumatic event. Each person faces unique stressors because of differences in age, phase of life, occupation, socio-economic status, personality and lifestyle.

Stress can also be specific or general. Both specific and general stress have been associated with health problems. For example, anxiety can feature prominently in chronic general stress and if this is coupled with certain physiological problems such as a weak heart, 'nervous' stomach, asthma, etc., it can be associated with various health problems. Furthermore, not only the intensity but also the duration of stress is important. If you should go for a driving test it would be normal to feel a bit stressed. This is specific stress which should be short term. During this period you focus your mind on the driving and the test, and a small amount of stress helps you to do your best. Afterwards you should calm down and feel less stressed. But if you should engage in an activity associated with unrelenting long-term stress-related problems, where your stress reaction persists, it could turn into chronic, long-term stress. But the individual uniqueness of the stress reaction is particularly linked to how you perceive and interpret situations (whether chronic or acute) and whether you have the ability to deal with them.

STRESS AND CHANGE

Like stress, change is part of human development. Although humankind has always been subjected to change, we currently live in times where change is prevalent more than ever before and at an unprecedented speed. Never before in our history have we had to cope with so much change. In fact, the only real constant left is that nothing is constant. Even if you should try to hang on to the old ways, you constantly change your reactions. Along with everything around you changing so rapidly all the time, you are expected to constantly meet the demands made on you and to adjust to change. Even the thinking parts of your brain have undergone a significant degree of change through evolution. This you can see, for example, in the frontal areas of the brain, your increase in knowledge, and the advancement of the brain to accommodate mathematics, language development and creativity. The brain is also responsible for intellectual functions, emotions, your perceptions, and your ability to anticipate the future or to dwell in the past, which often produce stress-provoking thoughts.

However, one thing that does not seem to have changed much is your physical reaction to stress. Because of this, it wouldn't be unreasonable to argue that, in a manner of speaking, physically you tend to use pre-historic weapons to fight the stress of today. Physically you are much the same as cavemen in your body's stress response, because the various systems in your body use the same mechanisms as way back then.

But psychologically, matters are different. Your body does not distinguish between real and imagined stress, but your changed and developed mind does. However, in today's stressful times, because you are faced with more psychological threats than ever before, every day you have to make more sense of what poses real stress and what doesn't. Furthermore, you tend to become sensitised to stress and respond to it like some people do to an allergy. Once you develop an allergy, such as to dust, and become sensitised to it, it takes only a little bit of it (or even just thinking about it) for you to start sneezing and to set off the 'biochemical alarm' that results in an attack of hay fever. So it is with becoming sensitised to stress. Once it becomes part of you, even minor stressors and irritations can trigger off a bigger stress reaction.

Another facet of this change is that not only does stress alter your psychological state, body and brain functions, but patterns of stressors themselves usually also change with time. Different phases of your life, and each era in time have their own stressor patterns. For example, as you enter the 21st century, stress patterns are vastly different from those of your ancestors. In modern times stress has become a buzzword associated with a range of causes covering reactions to rapid change, stock market crashes, technology and diseases like AIDS. Some of the more common modern stressors are discussed in Chapter 6. These were unknown when your forefathers were cave dwellers or lived in hunter-gatherer societies. They also experienced stress, such as exposure to vitamin and mineral deficiencies, possible starvation and malnutrition, lack of available clean water during droughts, hypothermia in winter, the risk of becoming a meal themselves when they were hunting for their next meal, worrying incessantly about the unknown, or lacking understanding of the forces of nature and science. They often had to literally fight off the stressor physically or run and hide when they were overwhelmed by life. But as stressful as such conditions were for them, modern society has clearly made things worse by creating an ever more demanding and competitive environment in which you have to survive. Worst of all, without warning and before they know it, stress literally sneaks up on some people and slowly squeezes the very life out of them. This is likely to get worse as we enter the new millennium, especially since we cannot always fight off the stressor or simply run away from it like our ancient ancestors did. In most instances, we have to learn new stress coping skills.

Likewise, by the time a person reaches late middle-age the stressor patterns have changed considerably from those associated with the demands of that person's teenage years because of the different needs and coping skills of different age groups. Other examples of changed stressor patterns are when a disease or an accident changes a person's life, or because of socio-economic changes. To complicate matters further, what you perceive as stressful today might produce quite a different perception tomorrow, regardless of severity. Therefore, time and the changes in stressor patterns that it brings, play an important role in your perception of stress and how you cope with it and vice versa.

All is not doom and gloom though, because the flip side of the coin tells another story as change brings with it bad as well as good. Not all change is bad for you, and not all stress is bad for you. Some change and some stress can be positive, desirable and necessary to your well-being. The good news is that it can make you grow psychologically, but the bad news is that being unable to cope with change and negative stress can cause serious health problems, disturb the balance in your life or even make you more accident-prone.

CONCLUSION

We use the word stress today almost casually, and while many people correctly assume that it is unavoidable, there are ways of harnessing its energy and of avoiding its damaging effects. In a sense, then, you face what might be termed the stress paradox. Stress is an essential part of life, but on the other hand it can be the cause of serious problems. On the upside, it forms the basis of the very energy needed to function optimally and to get you out of danger when necessary, but on the downside it can have harmful effects such as interpersonal conflict, reduced work performance, burnout, health problems and even danger to your life.

Stress is not always so much the villain, but more frequently it is the way you perceive and react to it. It is impossible, and even undesirable, to eliminate stress completely from your life. What is possible and desirable, though, is to reduce negative stress so that it does not drag you down and cause unhealthy physical, psychological or behavioural reactions. Since these reactions are, in part, based on how you see and evaluate the stress in your life, it is obvious that stress reactions will vary from person to person because different people will perceive the same situation differently. How stress is perceived depends on many factors, but in general people who seek help with stress do so because they realise that their coping skills are breaking down alarmingly. They need some other source of psychological empowerment or control.

SUMMARY OF THE MAIN PRINCIPLES

- Stress can be multifaceted, chronic (long-lasting) or acute (sudden and intense).
- There has always been and there always will be stress, which can affect anyone.
- Stress is your physiological, psychological and behavioural reactions when you attempt to adapt and adjust to internal and/or external demands, change or pressures that you cannot cope with.
- A stressor can be any event, situation, person, etc. that you perceive as stressful and induces your stress reaction.
- Knowledge about stress is a powerful stress management tool.
- Everything around you changes rapidly all the time, creating more demands to cope with. Even patterns of stressors change.
- Stress and change can be good and bad for you.
- You can become sensitised to stress. Once this has happened, it doesn't take much to trigger it off.
- Physically you react the same way to stress as people have always done. But, psychologically matters are different.
- It is not so much the stress and the change that are problematic, but the way you perceive and react to it.
- Recognising this and knowing what stress is, is your first step towards psychological self-empowerment and stress management.

CHAPTER 2

Understand why you feel keyed-up

STRESS AND THE NERVOUS SYSTEM

IN ORDER to understand the previous discussion of stress better you have to look at how the process of stress actually works. This response is a complex process that involves, amongst other things, the inter-relationship between your mind and body. Before considering the mechanisms involved in the stress response, let's briefly look at how the nervous system is organised, because it is involved in the very roots of stress-related behaviour. It consists of the central and peripheral nervous systems, simply illustrated in Figure 2.1. As can be seen, the central nervous system (the main control system of the body) includes the brain and the spinal cord.

STRESS AND THE BRAIN

The brain is the central executive organ of the nervous system (Figures 2.1 and 2.2). It used to be compared to a telephone switchboard in the past and more recently to a computer. It is neither, and even if switchboards and computers are wonderful inventions, they are not as extraordinary and complex as the brain. For example, the chief advantage of a computer is its amazing speed, but unlike the brain it cannot supply meaning and context to your world and lacks the unique ability to combine perceptions, thoughts, feelings and behaviour.

The brain is divided into various parts which perform different functions, a concept known as localisation of brain function. The cerebrum (the uppermost part of the forebrain) is itself also divided into two halves or cerebral hemispheres. These two hemispheres control opposite sides of the body and, although they are of similar structure, they have separate talents or areas of specialisation. They communicate with each other across a bundle of nerves called the corpus callossum. Studies have shown that language is mainly processed in the left hemisphere along with various kinds of logical and sequential tasks, such as solving mathematical problems and comprehending technical material. Some researchers also believe that this

11

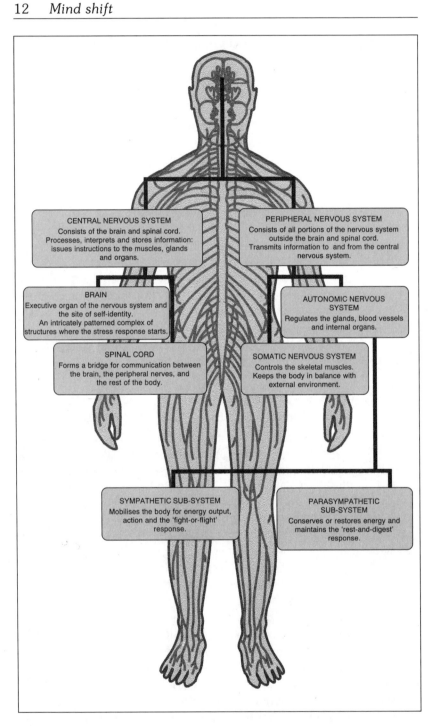

FIGURE 2.1   *The organisation of the nervous system.*

hemisphere explains actions and emotions outside of conscious awareness, including non-verbal ones. The right hemisphere seems better at problems that require visuo-spatial abilities (for example, reading a road map when you are planning a car journey or following a particular route or pattern), facial recognition (which involves recognising emotions expressed on the face), and appreciation of the arts and music. Its unique intellectual style also involves intuitive capabilities and the ability to see things as holistic. This is in direct contrast with the more analytical intellectual style of the left hemisphere, which is often favoured by traditional Western educational systems. The different intellectual styles have implications for stress management. However, even though the two hemispheres have different areas of specialisation, they function together in a naturally co-operative manner.

THE TWO PATHWAYS OF STRESS

It is useful to conceptualise the way we process stress-producing information as occurring via two basic pathways or routes – that is, the physiological and the psychological routes.

THE PHYSIOLOGICAL PATHWAY

This route involves the nervous system, but especially that part of the nervous system called the autonomic nervous system, shown in Figure 2.1. In the figure you can also see how the peripheral nervous system fits into the organisation of the whole nervous system, and how it links the rest of the body with the brain and the spinal cord. The portion that keeps the body in balance with the external environment (external homeostasis) is the somatic nervous system, and the part that maintains internal homeostasis makes up the autonomic nervous system, which features prominently in the stress response.

The autonomic nervous system

The autonomic nervous system largely participates in the involuntary activities of the body and controls, amongst other things, the heart, glands, blood vessels and the internal organs. It is called that because many of its actions are autonomous and self-regulatory, and it works more or less automatically. It is designed to continue its activities even when you are asleep. It is sub-divided into two chief components, the sympathetic and the parasympathetic sub-systems which are often

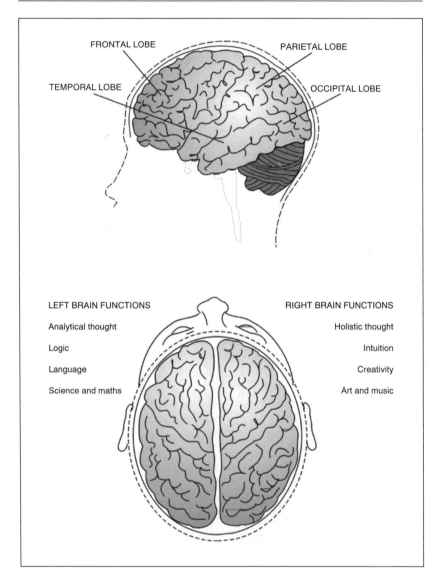

FIGURE 2.2   *The organisation of the brain.*

antagonistic or contrasting in their actions – they operate on the brake-accelerator principle similar to that found in cars. A normal state of your body is maintained by a balance between these two subsystems. One acts as a counterbalance to the other, and one part of the system slows down and reverses the effects of the other. In doing so, the sympathetic part acts as the accelerator and the parasympathetic as the brake.

The sympathetic sub-system

'I felt clammy, my hands and feet tingled, my heart was pounding so fast I thought it might burst out of my chest. I felt keyed up and began to experience a rapidness of breath. My muscles were so tense that they ached and my mind started racing,' so said Anne, a 33-year-old woman who described a classical stress reaction.

What occurred in the case of Anne was that the sympathetic part of her autonomic nervous system automatically kicked into action as her body reacted to stress. In this way, functioning as the accelerator, it geared her body for action. Although it operates continually, its effects are most dramatic during very stressful situations. This results in the 'fight-or-flight' response, first suggested by the noted American physiologist Walter B. Cannon, because it produces a number of different physiological changes in the body that make you more alert and active in a crisis situation that requires survival. In such a situation, your whole body gets prepared for action. It needs to make sure that the muscles are strong and well supplied with blood, sugar and oxygen. Even your digestive system prepares itself to supply energy by 'burning' sugar more quickly and foods that require long-term digestion, such as proteins and fat, less quickly. Your body even prepares to cope with tissue damage and additional blood platelets are produced to help the blood clot in case of injury, while your brain produces endorphines to block out immediate feelings of pain. Simultaneously, long-term immune system activity is repressed until the crisis is over. All this is designed to help your body produce and utilise energy rapidly so that you are ready to deal with the stressor physically – in the traditional, primitive manner. That is, your body is prepared for the 'fight-or-flight' response.

The parasympathetic sub-system

In contrast, the parasympathetic branch of the nervous system has been designed as a counterbalance to the sympathetic branch. That is why it is sometimes referred to as 'the rest-and-digest system' or the 'rest-and-recovery' phase. Its function is to conserve and restore energy and return you to the pre-action state once the stress has passed. It acts to decrease blood pressure and the rate of your heartbeat, and it stimulates your digestive system to process food. In the case of Anne mentioned earlier, it allowed her body to return to a more relaxed state after she had dealt with the stress.

Make the brake–accelerator principle work for you

Imagine your body's reaction to stress to be somewhat like a car you are driving which responds to acceleration and de-acceleration as in the brake–accelerator principle mentioned earlier. In a way then, the sympathetic sub-system functions like your car's accelerator (that is, it mobilises your body for action) and the parasympathetic sub-system functions like the car's brake when you want to decrease speed (it doesn't stop your body, but slows it down). Put differently, the sympathetic branch produces energy to deal with stress, whereas the parasympathetic branch helps you to conserve and store energy. Although they operate as opposites, the two sub-systems function together smoothly to orchestrate the numerous complex activities continuously taking place within the body, and also during the stress response.

Take the example of you having to avoid an accident when you're driving. You might have to suddenly increase speed and overtake a vehicle to avoid a collision, but once you've done this you decrease speed and slow down. When you attempt to avoid the collision, your nervous system's sympathetic branch increases your body's reactions such as your heart rate, breathing, reactions, etc. and when the stress has passed the parasympathetic branch slows down your body and keeps its rhythm regular and running smoothly again.

Just as you must stay in control of your vehicle to negotiate the traffic safely, so you must stay in control psychologically to cope effectively with stress as you negotiate life. To achieve this, good stress management includes psychological self-empowerment and positive self-management by striking an effective balance between your body's brake–accelerator control.

The role of the endocrine system

During the above process two things happened:

(a) a nervous system response which is short-lived; and
(b) an hormonal response which lasts longer and originates in the endocrine system.

Whereas the physiological changes involved in the 'fight-or-flight' response and a general state of arousal are stimulated by the neuronal impulses (chemical messengers) from the sympathetic sub-system of the autonomic nervous system, they are maintained by the action of the endocrine glands (derived from the Greek for 'secrete within') that form the endocrine system. This consists of a series of glands without ducts that secrete hormones to help regulate the activities of other tissues and organs, as illustrated in Figure 2.3. This figure shows the main glands responsible for the hormonal response, and represents a quick guided tour through the 'power station' behind your stress response. Hormones (derived from the Greek 'to urge on') are chemical substances that act as long-distance messengers because they are produced in one part of the body but have an affect far away from their origin. They are 'pumped' directly into the blood stream and then travel to other organs and cells which they influence. They have many different functions, and some are activated by the nervous system response. On the other hand, they in turn affect the functioning of the nervous system.

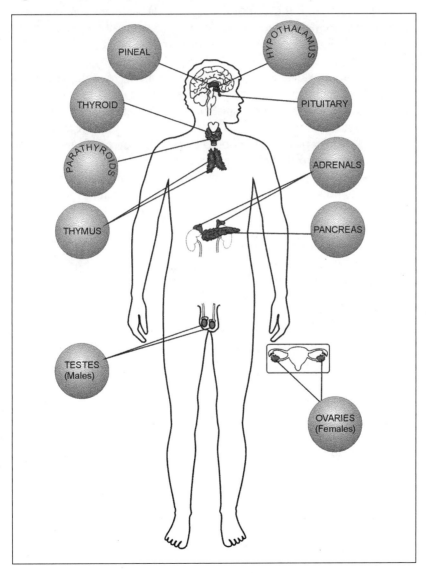

FIGURE 2.3   *The power station behind it all.*

THE PSYCHOLOGICAL PATHWAY

This brings us to the second route or the psychological pathway by which you process stress-related information. It involves your perception of the stress in your life, including your assessment and appraisal of whether the stress is inappropriate and harmful to you or whether it is appropriate and necessary so that you can function optimally (that is, at a level which is most favourable or advantageous to you and that produces the best possible result). To achieve this, you need to answer two basic questions: 'Is the stress positive and to your advantage?' or 'Is it negative and to your disadvantage?' Naturally, the thinking part of your brain (including your decision-making abilities) and coping skills are very important in this process. Also, to be able to answer these questions successfully, you need to have knowledge about the stress in your life and how you are affected by it.

Take the example of the car again. If you find yourself in a particularly tricky traffic situation that could be potentially very stressful, your perception of the traffic situation (stressor), how you evaluate it, and your driving and decision-making skills will all determine how well you do, and how effectively you cope with the stress produced by the situation.

The stress cascade

Your reaction during the stress response produces an automatic reaction in your body (the physiological pathway). It takes place stepwise, almost like a cascade where the previous step or phase affects the next one. This is also influenced by your perception and appraisal of the stressor and your resources to cope with it (the psychological pathway). In brief, Figure 2.4 gives you some idea of how the biochemistry and physiology of the stress response works.

The problem

Many modern cars sound off a buzzer or flashing dash light to signal or warn you if something is wrong or requires attention. This happens, for example, when your car is low on fuel or when you leave the lights on after parking it. Once you have attended to the problem, the warning signal stops. If you are a careful driver, you shouldn't have such problems too often. Your body and psyché also trigger off warning signs when your stress becomes a problem. However, a major problem is that in modern society these physiological and psychological warning signals or alarm mechanisms tend to flash or chime too often and are repeatedly ignored. An additional rub lies in the fact that when you are confronted with stress in your life and you

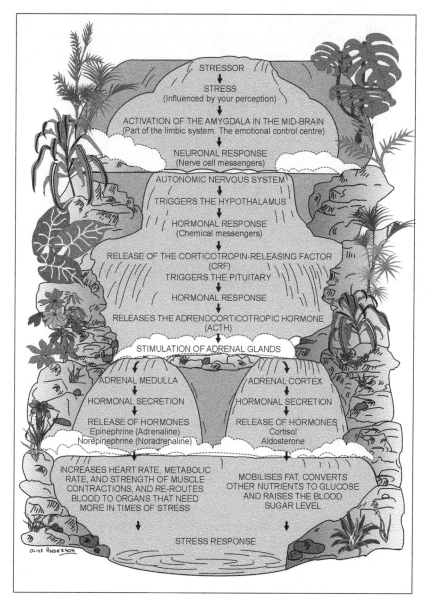

FIGURE 2.4   *The stress cascade.*

get into that activated or arousal state brought on by the sympathetic branch of the autonomic nervous system, it is frequently not possible to either fight the stress or to run away from it, which would be the natural 'fight-or-flight' response. In the environment where you tend to experience the stress (work, home or society), you usually have to stay and face it. If such stress is then not adequately resolved you stay in a high state of activation or arousal for an inordinate length of time, resulting in elevated, extended and protracted periods of stress. If this situation is allowed to continue, it means that your parasympathetic, and subsequently the 'rest-and-digest' phase, gets very little chance to come into play as it should naturally.

Take the example of driving a car again. If you end up speeding out of control and you don't heed any external (road signs, traffic lights, etc.) or internal signals (warning lights, buzzers, etc.), the end result could be disastrous. Or, if on a very hot day the radiator water starts boiling and you continue to ignore the warning signals on the dashboard, the car's engine could seize up. Likewise, if your stress levels persist and accelerate out of control, the result can be a devastating effect on your physical and mental well-being. Or, like the car's engine seizing up, you could end up with burnout. If you cannot fight or run away from the stress and are forced to stay and face it, what do you do? You learn the stress management skills which are detailed in this book.

Health-risk behaviour and lifestyle diseases

Don't forget, though, that just as the condition you keep your car in will play a role in how it serves you, so the condition that you keep your body and mind in is important in dealing with stress. This means living a healthy lifestyle and avoiding health-risk behaviours. Lifestyle diseases (or the so-called diseases of 'choice' that people develop because of the way they live) and health-risk behaviours have been identified as major sources of concern that require high priority in today's world. There are a host of lifestyle diseases and health-risk behaviours associated with stress in one way or another. Typical ones include those that result from substance abuse (such as smoking, alcohol, medicine and drug abuse), dietary deficiencies, violence, and the neglect or abuse of children and spouses or partners.

Other common examples include road rage and reckless or irresponsible driving behaviour. I often quote driving behaviour in this book to illustrate certain issues about stress because it is such an obvious and prevalent behaviour that affects so many people. The ripple effects of road accidents go much further than the injuries caused to the occupants of vehicles and pedestrians when one considers the stress caused to surviving relatives and friends, and the enormous financial implications that result from accidents. I also use driving behaviour to illustrate certain points about human behaviour because motor vehicles (including motor cycles) sometimes take on a psychological meaning for the owners that goes far beyond the original reason for which they were invented (Figure 2.5). For example, apart from being used in sport (racing, etc.) and entertainment (stunts, chases in movies, etc.), they are often used as status or other psychological symbols, or serve as an extension of personal space, or as an ego booster, or as a means to 'act out' stress and frustration. For some, getting into another's vehicle can acquire an intimate encroachment on the physical space boundaries of the vehicle's owner. It provides plenty of opportunity for touching or even 'accidental' touching. On the other hand, the inside of cars is frequently where most of the 'action' takes place between couples who are courting. There is also an element of trust involved that other drivers, passengers and pedestrians place in the drivers of vehicles regarding their own safety.

FIGURE 2.5 *Don't drive your body like a car out of control.*

CONCLUSION

The nervous system is at the basis of the stress response. This includes:

(a) a sub-conscious and physiological action; and
(b) a conscious and psychological or voluntary action which relies heavily on your perception and other psychological factors.

In other words, the reasons why you feel so keyed-up following the stress response can be usefully understood from both a physiological/biochemical point of view (or pathway), and a psychological one. Both pathways interact closely. The essence of this book is specifically concerned with this second pathway – the psychological and conscious route of processing stress-related information and how it affects your body and mind. This whole process also involves your social environment and lifestyle.

SUMMARY OF THE MAIN PRINCIPLES

- The stress response is a complex process that involves the inter-relationship between mind and body.
- It occurs through both a physiological and psychological pathway or route.
- The physiological route involves the autonomic nervous system, which is part of the central nervous system. It is further sub-divided into the sympathetic and the parasympathetic sub-systems.
- The sympathetic sub-system gears the body for action through nerve cell (neuronal) and chemical (hormonal) messengers.
- This triggers hormones and a stress cascade in the body, and prepares it for the 'fight-or-flight' response.
- The parasympathetic sub-system is a counterbalance to the sympathetic sub-system. It conserves and restores energy. This prepares the body for the 'rest-and-digest' phase.
- The psychological route involves your perception of stress, your thinking processes and your coping skills.
- The physiological and psychological routes interact closely. Your social environment and lifestyle play important roles in the stress process.

CHAPTER 3

Good and bad stress

NOT ALL STRESS IS BAD FOR YOU

A DEGREE of stress often spurs you on to achieve more by providing the energy and motivation for you to do your best. The eminent pioneer in stress research, Canadian physician Hans Selye, called such positive stress eustress. He devised the concept of the General Adaptation Syndrome (GAS) which has three phases that illustrate the basic stress response as seen in Figure 3.1.

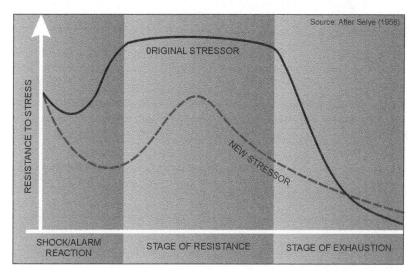

FIGURE 3.1 *Three stages of coping with stress. When already coping with one long-term stressor, it is even more difficult to cope with a new stressor.*

In stage one of the GAS (the alarm phase) you are in a general state of arousal or activation, but with no specific organ being negatively affected yet. This allows you to fight or flee (the 'fight-or-flight' response). For example, when you are driving a car, this stage prepares you to deal with a difficult traffic situation.

In stage two, your body becomes used to stress if it continues for a long enough period and you can't avoid it. This is called the adaptation phase or phase of resistance. During this phase your body's physiological responses are above normal which makes you more susceptible to further stress. An example might be a difficult traffic situation ending up in a traffic jam. If your body has mobilised to fight off the stress of the traffic congestion and its consequences and that lasts for hours, you could be more easily irritated by other minor frustrations (stressors) caused by your perception of the behaviour of other motorists or the traffic officers who are struggling to bring the traffic flow back to normal. Or, just think how irritable you might be when you don't feel well and your car gets a flat tyre on a hot day. How will you react if this happens in the midst of the traffic jam? In this second phase the body adapts to cope with the presence of stress for an indefinite period. The stress response is channelled to the specific organ system most capable of dealing with it or of suppressing it.

However, such adaptation energy is limited and if the stress persists it could overwhelm your body's resources and deplete it of energy. Then you enter into the third stage (referred to as the phase of exhaustion). During this last phase the organ system responsible for dealing with the stress breaks down and you become vulnerable to more serious physical and psychological problems. Those reactions that originally allowed your body to resist short-term stressors during the first stage (for example, increased energy, tensing of muscles in readiness for action, increase in blood pressure, etc.) can in the last stage become unhealthy and bad for you. For example, your tense muscles can result in pain and persistent elevated blood pressure can contribute to hypertension, or some of the other stress-related disorders can ultimately develop, or you could completely lose control.

Therefore, although some stress can be positive, most of us are not supposed to be able to withstand prolonged, negative stress. We tend to function best when positive stress (or energy) is used. When survival calls for it, however, we are all capable of keeping up short bursts of high energy levels to deal with emergency demands in order to successfully defend against or escape from the threat that causes the stress (the 'fight-or-flight' response). As you have seen, this activation or arousal is automatically produced by the sympathetic branch of the autonomic nervous system (the accelerator). When the threat subsides, the activation or arousal dissipates as a result of the function of the parasympathetic branch of the autonomic nervous system (the brake). We now re-adjust to the resting or normal state (the pre-arousal state) – we have applied our psychological brakes to slow down. If, however, we don't (or can't) do this and continue in the high level energy output of the sympathetic arousal state, physical and psychological problems eventually arise.

When we considered the stress paradox earlier on, we saw that the physiological (body) response is a fairly basic one. If we consider this autonomic nervous system response objectively, it seems that in the process of evolution we have changed little physiologically to help us adapt to the stress of the modern world, since we tend to respond to modern stress in the same way as humans (or animals) have always done. However, the thinking parts of our brain have changed considerably during evolution. Unlike animals, for example, we can anticipate the future, which is often the basis of stress caused by anticipatory anxiety (excessive worry about what might happen), or we can produce irrational thoughts from past experiences that can cause current or future stress. On the other hand, because we also have reasoning abilities and rational deductive thinking capacities, the good news is that we can utilise these to cope better with stress.

Because of this, your perception of the stressor, your thought processes and coping skills could affect your eventual stress response, and determine whether you experience good or bad stress. The secret is to decide 'what is healthy and what is unhealthy stress for you?' Not all stress can (or should be) avoided, nor should you aim for the impossible goal of a stress-free life. Take the example of the car again. You know that it gradually wears out and your aim should not be to get rid of such normal wear and tear altogether, but rather to minimise it. Likewise, you should not strive to avoid all stress but rather learn how to recognise negative stress and then deal with it. One sure way to minimise damage to your car is to look after it and to drive it carefully. In the same way you can minimise stress by looking after yourself and leading a healthy lifestyle. In this process, you should accept that some stress is necessary and can be positive. Just as the car you are driving needs extra fuel when you sometimes have to accelerate to make it go faster, so you need positive stress and extra energy to do your best in certain situations. This book is not directed at positive or eustress, but it is more concerned with excessive and unhealthy stress or distress.

SOME PEOPLE ARE LESS STRESS-PRONE

There are wide individual differences in the amount of stress that a person can cope with before it becomes a problem. Just as one driver might be better than another at negotiating heavy traffic, so one person may consider a specific stressor positive, while another person may perceive such stress as negative. It is an individual situation. So, always look at your stress response relative to yourself rather than to others.

Modern health psychologists emphasise that we should be interested in what generates and maintains health, thereby using a salutogenic approach (salute means health). From the point of view of stress management, such a health-centred approach wants answers to questions such as, 'how come some people who should by all accepted standards succumb to stress, don't?', 'how come some even flourish under what others would perceive to be negative stressful conditions?', 'how can healthy people remain well, not succumb to the ravages of stress, and learn to possibly even turn stress to their advantage?', and 'how does all this relate to the concept of well-being?' Two ways of finding answers to such penetrating questions are to study those people who seem to have high stress levels and should become sick but don't because they cope well with their stress, and those who claim they experience benign (unharmful) stress.

In the light of this, let's reconsider the paradox of stress, especially the question of stress and change. Some of the changes in life to which we are exposed result in only minor stress, whereas others bring major stress. Psychologists have been slow to define benign stress, but most of us have experienced it. Take, for example, the excitement and competitive life in a city. Although behind 'the energy' of the city lies tension and stress that impose enormous pressures on some people, for others the returns of city life can be exciting and have exhilarating compensations such as good facilities, recognition for achievements, access to beautiful shopping malls, museums, theatres, libraries, sporting facilities, and places for fun seeking. To some people, the 'fast lane' can even be an attraction in itself associated with little stress, and some revel in the busy life of the city.

There is evidence that some people may not react as negatively to stress that would floor most other people. Certain people are even active stress-seekers, almost as if their stress-response becomes an addictive experience in itself. Some of them have been referred to as 'stimulus addicts'. They seem to get an emotional lift from their stress-seeking behaviour. It has also been shown that 'stress-resistant people' often have what has been referred to as a kind of psychological hardiness. People with 'hardy' personalities tend to have a strong sense of coherence, commitment, challenge and control. For them, hardiness is an important stress reducer and life is manageable. On the other hand, in as much as some people are stress-seekers, others are stress-prone. That is, their general make-up and lifestyle make them more prone to stress than what would otherwise have been the case.

Given all this, the question that begs an answer of course is: 'Can you do something to become less stress-prone or to cope better with stress?' The answer is an unqualified 'Yes!'

THE STRESS CURVE

Look at the illustration of the stress curve in Figure 3.2. Your position on this stress curve is dynamic and varied and the shape of the curve differs from one person to the next. Where you fit depends on a whole range of factors: your coping mechanisms, how much stress you can comfortably handle, your constitutional make-up, diet, level of fitness, personality characteristics, thoughts and many other factors, but most importantly your perception of the stressors in your life, your thought processes and what you believe you can do about it. Also, don't forget that sometimes the very methods you use when you are under stress (the 'fight-or-flight' response, fear, anger, etc.) can turn out to be the very coping mechanisms that give you most trouble, because your actual response to stress can be more painful psychologically or physically than the stress itself.

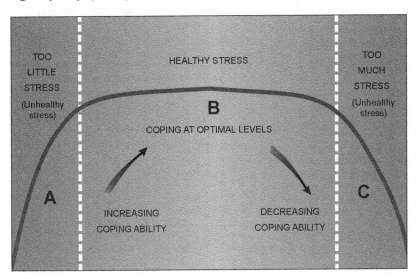

FIGURE 3.2   *The stress curve. A healthy lifestyle increases the ability to cope better with stress.*

On this curve you can see that not only over-stress but also under-stress can be equally bad for you. So boredom, lack of stimulation and a very laid back, lethargic, inactive lifestyle can also be unhealthy. Although your level of performance improves with increasing amounts of stress, this increase cannot continue indefinitely (A). When you pass the peak of your position on the stress curve (B), your health and performance are negatively affected (C). If you experience too much stress, your adaptive energy can become exhausted. This can result in all sorts of problems, because negative stress causes chemical changes in your brain which can affect the clinical and hormonal balance of your body. Likewise, too little stress for too long can be a problem that also affects your well-being, because neither severe overload nor severe underload can be tolerated for too long. The point is to stay out of the negative phase on either end of the stress curve and to focus on positive stress.

POSITIVE STRESS CAN LEAD TO . . .

- good concentration
- co-operative behaviour
- maintaining high standards
- effective problem-solving skills
- good self- and time management
- good communication skills
- clear and confident decision-making skills
- assertiveness
- less aggressiveness and submissiveness
- supportive and harmonious relationships
- good work attendance
- a positive, happy and cheerful manner
- increased optimism
- concern for others
- better coping skills
- an appropriate sense of humour
- enhanced achievements and high productivity
- a strong interest in life
- good long-term planning
- clear thinking
- a high level of motivation
- improved self-esteem
- improved self-confidence
- realistic perceptions and self-expectations
- increased energy
- feeling valued by others
- flowing with change
- a balanced and healthy lifestyle
- general wellness and a healing image
- more time for fun and relaxation

SENSORY AND PERCEPTUAL DEPRIVATION AND STRESS

The absence of stress can in a way be stressful. Such deprivational stress is usually associated with lack of stimulation and associated factors such as loneliness, insufficient intellectual or emotional challenges, depression or other psychological problems, concentration difficulties, loss of self-esteem, repetitive behaviour and boredom. For example, emotional deprivation in the young can severely affect happiness and well-being, and being deprived of stimulation (including physical and mental exercise) can play havoc with their well-being. Young babies who are exposed to long periods of emotional deprivation or who don't receive stimulation do not thrive and often have poor motor, speech and social development. Research has shown that at the other end of the age spectrum, the chances of heart attacks are significantly increased in the first two years of retirement, especially if retirement is associated with a sedentary lifestyle and lack of new experiences.

At the extreme end of the scale, sensory and perceptual deprivation resulting in severe withdrawal from stimulation (light, sound, taste, touch, smell, etc.) can lead to high distress levels, unrealistic fears, psychotic-like symptoms including hallucinations, and other serious psychological complications. Controlled laboratory experiments with adult and animal subjects have demonstrated many of the ill-effects of such severe sensory and perceptual deprivation, which occur because the nervous system needs a constant level of stimulation to function normally.

STRESS AND BRAINWASHING

Brainwashing (a term coined by George Orwell in his novel *1984*) often forms the basis of severe deprivation whereby the tactics of isolation, thought control and political conditioning are commonly used. One must make a distinction between brainwashing and propaganda. In propaganda, slogans and exortations are repeatedly used, for example, during a public crisis to get people to accept the propaganda message. In brainwashing the focus is on an extreme distortion of mental processes during which the 'victim's' guilt is frequently exploited. Classically the person is deprived of basic needs like sleep, nourishment and privacy and is made overtly dependent on those who are trying to do this. The purpose is to wear the 'victim' down in order to create a susceptibility during which thoughts and beliefs can be changed through continuous persuasion and exhausting interrogation under very uncomfortable conditions. Clearly this can be an enormously stressful experience.

A related concept is derived from an incident during a bank robbery in Stockholm (Sweden) years ago. In this incident a woman was held captive for some 131 hours, during which she 'fell in love' with one of the robbers. This was an inappropriate 'defence' against the stress caused by her ordeal. In such cases, 'victims' who are held captive can become highly stressed and even fear that they might lose their lives at any moment. This can result in irrational thoughts, feelings and behaviour and possibly even a child-like trust in and dependence on the 'captors'. During this period the 'victims' can even identify with the cause of the 'captors' in order to cope with their own stress-related feelings of helplessness at being trapped in the situation. In a way the 'victims' begin to see their 'captors' as 'good' and those who try to rescue them (the real good people) without conceding to the demands of the 'captors' as 'bad'. It can take months for these effects to wear off once the 'victims' have been freed and the stress associated with the traumatic ordeal is being treated. Sometimes there can be enduring negative effects for many years. This type of response has been noticed by researchers in many hostage situations, and has come to be known as the 'Stockholm Syndrome'.

Lately, reports about cults and the behaviour of their members have been much in the news and questions have been asked why intelligent, emotionally stable people become involved to the point of being exploited by some movements. A good example of this is the story of the cult movement 'The People's Temple', founded by Jim Jones, who got his followers to implicitly believe that he was their 'Dad' and 'Saviour'. In the 1970s he set up a 'colony' called 'Jonestown' in a remote part of Guyana that he promoted as a 'religious utopia'. Through continuous brainwashing and various other techniques that included social isolation, abuse and hardship his 'utopia' ended up more like life in a concentration camp and eventually led to a total disaster – mass suicide committed by drinking cyanide-laced Kool-Aid (a beverage). This is a prime example where taking absolute control of other people's minds resulted in their total destruction.

Many terms have been used to describe the techniques used in the battle for the mind such as: brainwashing; deprogramming; coercive persuasion; indoctrination; thought reform; operant conditioning; classical conditioning; snapping; ideological reconstruction; ideological remoulding; and menticide (mind killing). These can involve various approaches, but authorities generally agree that, more often than not, few mysterious or unusual forces are at play and that a technique for thought changing (called cognitive restructuring) usually forms the basis of altering people's ordinary thought processes, although other activities might also be used. However, the trauma of being held captive – whether by criminals, terrorists or whoever – can produce stress levels in the 'victims' that can make their normal thoughts, beliefs and emotions extremely vulnerable to irrational actions.

CONCLUSION

In summary, the stress reaction is natural and normal. It occurs quickly and automatically for you to perform optimally. If the stress is negative, prolonged and intense, however, and you cannot cope with it effectively, the result is disruption of your health and/or normal life and routine. Such unhealthy stress can be specific, acute or chronic and cause unpleasant physical or psychological effects, or even result in medical or psychological disorders. According to the General Adaption Syndrome (GAS), the stress response can occur in three phases: the alarm phase, the adaptation phase and the phase of exhaustion.

Eustress or optimal (positive) stress occurs when an increase in stress is associated with an increase in health and performance. Distress (negative stress) occurs when your stress levels go beyond optimal stress and continue to increase, causing your health and performance to decrease.

Stress, like change, is necessary for development and progress. It can be a positive growth factor, but it can also be a negative force if excessive and too much for you to handle, and if your ability to cope is surpassed. The two cardinal issues here are: the intensity and duration of stress, and your adaptability. Good stress management means harnessing the energy of healthy stress and minimising the consequences of unhealthy stress.

SUMMARY OF THE MAIN PRINCIPLES

- Not all stress is bad for you, because the stress reaction is natural and normal.
- Positive stress can spur you on to achieve your best or to help you deal with an emergency.
- You are not designed to be exposed to prolonged negative stress, which can be very harmful.
- The basic stress response based on the General Adaptation Syndrome has three phases: the alarm phase which puts you in a state of general arousal; the adaptation phase during which your physiological responses are above normal and you are more susceptible to other stress; and the exhaustion phase where you become vulnerable to serious physical and psychological problems.
- Some people flourish on stress and some are even stress-seekers. They enjoy the 'fast lane'.
- Some people have hardy personalities. They tend to have a strong sense of challenge and control and their hardiness helps them to reduce stress.
- Some stress is good for you, too little stress is bad for you, and too much stress is also bad for you.
- You have to decide what constitutes healthy or unhealthy stress for you, and how to use stress to work for you and not against you.

Part Two

How stress affects you

To understand how stress affects you, you need to know the impact it has on you physically, psychologically and socially, as well as how to identify your own stress levels and the sources of stress in your own life.

CHAPTER 4

Stress and the mind–body connection

THE HOLISTIC APPROACH

STRESS management should include changing any perceptions of the mind–body split you may still support. Instead of perceiving the mind and body as separate entities you should be concerned with how they function as one, and how one affects the other. This ultimately impacts on your total functioning and well-being, and your improved ability to cope with stress. You cannot separate the two in caring for your health generally, but especially not in the process of dealing with stress. Your mind and body function as a unit. For example, when you are stressed you may feel a lack of self-confidence (mind) and show physiological symptoms such as muscle tension (body). Curing one won't eliminate the other. Dealing with them both in the context of stress management will. Likewise, the social part of your functioning (which includes the spiritual component of your life, however you conceive that) and the need to place greater emphasis on quality of life cannot be ignored in this process.

In addition, in stress management there is a need to be person-focused rather than disease-focused, and to accept the role of stress in psychological or physical disorders as a reality. Health cannot be viewed from a purely medical, psychological or social point of view, but should be seen as a marriage of the three. This is in line with the biopsychosocial approach which is based on the principle that biological, psychological and social forces closely interact and affect your health. Failure to cope at any of these levels may seriously increase your vulnerability to stress. Health is not simply the absence of disease. It is a complete state of physical, psychological and social well-being. People in general function best when they optimise all three.

In this holistic approach there has been a perceptual shift away from a 'pure' medical or 'psychological' model or the view that diseases are caused by single factors. A different view is taken – that diseases are caused by many things, including an unhealthy lifestyle full of high stress levels. This development can be seen as a kind of a counterbalance to the tendency to compartmentalise health and disease into neat little packages. In a sense it has similarities to the traditional 'folk models' of health and disease seen in traditional African societies. In many ways traditional healers have always practised such a system, because they have long recognised the significance of incorporating all aspects of human functioning into their treatment programmes and, unlike some Western approaches, do not place their patients and their diseases into neat compartments. An estimated 80 per cent of African patients who consult a Western trained doctor also consult a traditional healer. Traditional healers form an integral part of African culture and communities and have been doing so since time immemorial. They fulfil functions which go way beyond those of the bio-medically trained Western health care consultant, and are available in areas where Western technology is not always available. They enhance the quality of health care using a community-based approach, and their practices are based on knowledge and beliefs which existed long before the development of modern scientific medicine. Their patients' illness, behaviour and the health services traditional healers offer in their communities reveal their own and their patients' perceptions of mind and body, and the inter-relationship between them is seen as holistic. Any form of stress management that ignores this is psychologically unsatisfactory.

MEDICAL PROBLEMS AND STRESS

The expression 'stress can kill' has been supported by a growing body of research. You may have noticed the connection between stress and physical illness in your own life, or you may have seen how someone's health takes a turn for the worse when they have been exposed to high stress levels. A lot of people suffer because no one believes that their 'physical' symptoms are manifestations of stress. Also, a lot of medical patients find it hard to understand how stress can cause physical symptoms. This link has a lot to do with the relationship between stress, immune function and disease as discussed further on in this chapter.

Many authorities have shown that in general, psychological or behavioural factors may play a potential role in the presentation or treatment of almost every general medical condition and may precipitate or worsen many of their symptoms by eliciting stress-related physiological responses. Nevertheless, certain specific medical conditions are known where psychological factors affect the condition. These are sometimes called 'psychosomatic' disorders. The list in Table 4.1 is more comprehensive than what is understood by psychosomatic disorders, but gives some idea of the range of medical problems that are affected by psychological factors and stress.

STRESS AND DISEASE

Not only can stress be related to lifestyles but also to the development, aggravation and maintenance of a number of health problems. Surveys show that approximately 60 per cent to 90 per cent of all patient visits to physicians in general practice are directly or indirectly related to psychological factors. Of these, stress-related conditions make up a significant proportion. Stress can indirectly influence health outcomes in many different ways. For example, exposure to unhealthy stress can lead to accidents that adversely affect health, and the Japanese (renowned for their work performance) use the term karoshi to denote a condition that results from over-work and stress that can result in disease. Stress can also occur as a response to disease itself, or to its treatment. The type, meaning and the significance of a particular disease usually determines the degree of stress invoked in the person with the disease and in that person's family. Stress, therefore, should not only be related to the cause of a particular disease, but can be a common response to the disease and its treatment. There is also a well-demonstrated relationship between stress, emotion and disease. Although emotions are difficult to define, they are increasingly being recognised as entities in their own right and there is abundant evidence of their role in disease.

Sometimes stress-related (psychological factors) can affect (aggravate) an existing medical condition, and at other times initiate or contribute to its cause, or perpetuate it. Whether stress plays a role in the origin, worsening or continuation of medical conditions, or how it affects their progression is not always clear and probably varies from condition to condition and person to person. More research in this regard is being done all the time. What is known, is that because there are wide individual differences in people's ability to cope with stress, a negative response to stress can result from an interaction of several variables. These can include the genetic and constitutional (physical inheritance and psychological endowment) make-up of the person, as well as environmental factors, which may tax the person's coping mechanisms and lifestyle and may result in health-risk behaviour.

The following two examples illustrate how inordinate (excessive) stress can be an important factor in physical conditions. Firstly, when you are exposed to stress it causes your muscles to contract. There are three types of muscles in your body: smooth, skeletal and cardiac muscles. Although they have different functions, they also have

TABLE 4.1

HEALTH PROBLEMS AFFECTED BY PSYCHOLOGICAL FACTORS AND STRESS	
✓ ACNE	DISEASE)
✓ ADDISON'S DISEASE	✓ HYPERVENTILATION
✓ ALLERGIC REACTIONS	SYNDROME
✓ AMENORRHEA	✓ HYPOGLYCAEMIA
✓ ANGINA PECTORIS	✓ INFECTIOUS DISEASES
✓ ANGIONEUROTIC OEDEMA	✓ IRRITABLE COLON
✓ ARRYTHMIA	✓ LUPUS ERYTHEMATOSUS
✓ ARTHRITIS	✓ MIGRAINE
✓ ASTHMATIC WHEEZING	✓ MYOSITIS (LUMBAGO)
✓ AUTOIMMUNE DISEASES	✓ MUCOUS COLITIS
✓ BACKACHE	✓ MUSCULAR SPASM DISEASE
✓ BRONCHIAL ASTHMA	✓ NAUSEA
✓ CANCER	✓ NEURODERMATITIS
✓ CARDIOSPASM	✓ OBESITY
✓ CARDIAC ARRHYTHMIA	✓ PAIN
✓ CARDIOVASCULAR DISEASE	✓ PAINFUL MENSTRUATION
✓ COLDS	✓ PEPTIC ULCERS
✓ CORONARY HEART DISEASE	✓ PRURITUS ANI
✓ CROHN'S DISEASE (CHRONIC	✓ PYLOROSPASM
INFLAMMATORY BOWEL	✓ RAYNAUD'S DISEASE
DISEASE)	✓ REGIONAL ENTERITIS
✓ CUSHING'S SYNDROME	✓ RHEUMATOID ARTHRITIS
✓ DERMATITIS	✓ SACROILIAC PAIN
✓ DIABETES MELLITUS	✓ SEXUAL DISORDERS
✓ DUODENAL ULCER	✓ SKIN DISEASES, SUCH AS
✓ ECZEMA	PSORIASIS
✓ EPILEPSY	✓ SPASTIC COLITIS
✓ EPSTEIN-BARR VIRUS	✓ SUPPRESSION OF THE IMMUNE
(MONONUCLEOSIS)	SYSTEM
✓ ESSENTIAL HYPERTENSION	✓ TACHYCARDIA
✓ GASTRIC ULCERS	✓ TUBERCULOSIS
✓ GASTROINTESTINAL	✓ ULCERATIVE COLITIS
PATHOLOGY	✓ URETHRITIS (BACTERIAL AND
✓ HEADACHE	CHRONIC YEAST)
✓ HERPES	✓ URTICARIA
✓ HIVES	✓ VOMITING
✓ HYPERINSULINISM	✓ WARTS
✓ HYPERTHYROIDISM (GRAVES'	

certain things in common from a stress point of view, that is, stress affects them, they have the ability to contract, and if the stress is severe and lasts for a long time they can go into muscular spasm. This can result in pain, disease and even sudden death – depending on the location, duration and severity of the muscle contraction or spasm. The smooth muscles are generally present in the walls of hollow organs, for example, in the oesophagus, stomach, duodenum, colon, urinary tract, along the walls of the arteries and airway passages of the lungs. They are not under voluntary control. The skeletal muscles are attached, amongst others, to the skeleton, causing the bones to move when they contract. The skeletal muscles are under voluntary control and you can therefore contract them when you want to. The last type (cardiac muscles) are found in the heart and they are also not under voluntary control. One of their key characteristics is their rhythmic contractions and they are at particular risk from stress, which is made worse if the person has heart problems. Clearly, if any of these muscle groups malfunction as a result of stress, the health consequences can be serious.

Secondly, the skin is the largest organ of the body and one of the first to show the ravages of the stress response. Because the skin is frequently a target organ for excessive stress, several dermatological conditions are associated with psychological factors such as acne, herpes simplex, eczema, psoriasis, urticaria (which has been referred to as suppressed weeping), etc. Some authorities have found that up to 40 per cent or more of skin disorders are associated with stress. In some cases stress causes these disorders, in others stress makes them worse, and yet in others skin disorders cause stress because of the unpleasant psychological and social consequences of unsightly skin disorders. This can negatively affect body image.

STRESS AND YOUR IMMUNE SYSTEM

The word 'immune' is derived from Latin, meaning 'safe'. The body's immune response depends on its ability to distinguish between the body itself and foreign matter (for example, viruses). Our thoughts and emotions affect our immune defences, and it is well known that the relationship between stress and the immune system can range from such diverse conditions as the common cold to certain types of cancer. Because it is so important for the prevention and cure of a wide range of different diseases, the immune system can be seen as the body's own surveillance system which serves to protect the body from various attacks on its normal body tissue. Stress can make the immune system function less efficiently, leaving the body open to 'attack'. A person with low (suppressed) immunity tends to have less ability to resist or fight disease, especially certain types of infectious diseases. High stress levels can, therefore, increase susceptibility to diseases such as colds, flu and other viral infections. This is because the immune system is designed to defend the body against foreign invaders and to recognise foreign substances such as flu viruses, bacteria, and even certain tumour cells and to destroy or deactivate them.

To do this, the immune system employs various weapons – specific types of cells, for example, natural killer cells which are a type of lymphocyte specialised to recognise and kill tumour cells and other foreign bodies. Prolonged stress can suppress these cells, weakening the immune system's ability to fight disease and infection. The person's immunity is suppressed by stress in proportion to the intensity of the stress. For example, commonly quoted psychosocial stressors in this regard include loss, bereavement, depression, prolonged separation from a loved one and relentless work pressure. There is some evidence that acute (short-term) stress appears to be less of an immunosuppressor than long-term stress, but lots of little stressors added up can lead to chronic (long-term) stress that does impede immune function.

CELLS IN IMMUNE RESPONSES

There are several types of cells that are important in immune responses. For example, two basic kinds of white cells in the immune system are the lymphocytes whose primary function is to recognise and destroy foreign cells, and the phagocytes whose primary function is to ingest and eliminate them. Natural killer (NK) cells are a type of lymphocyte and are important in cancer (tumour) detection and rejection. NK cells also recognise body cells that have been altered by viruses in order to quickly destroy them. Stress can affect these functions.

It is important to know that there is also a positive relationship between psychological factors and good health. Plenty of research has shown that positive thinking, positive emotions, an optimistic attitude and a healthy psychological environment can strengthen the immune system's ability to fight disease, and can help with rapid recovery when disease does strike.

CONCLUSION

In summary, there is converging evidence that the mind and body interact to protect your health. When we consider the psychological consequences or symptoms of stress later on, remember that the stress reaction can intimately affect all the bodily functions listed in Table 4.2.

This knowledge of stress and the mind–body connection has lead to the development of various psychological techniques for the treatment of stress, including those discussed in this book.

TABLE 4.2

BODILY FUNCTIONS THAT CAN BE AFFECTED BY STRESS
✓ PERCEPTUAL SENSES
✓ NERVOUS SYSTEM
✓ HORMONAL BALANCE
✓ CARDIOVASCULAR SYSTEM
✓ DIGESTIVE SYSTEM
✓ RESPIRATORY FUNCTION
✓ UROGENITAL SYSTEM
✓ SKIN
✓ IMMUNE SYSTEM

SUMMARY OF THE MAIN PRINCIPLES

- The mind and body do not function as separate entities, but holistically.
- The social and spiritual components of your life are important in this process.
- It is important to be person-focused rather than disease-focused.
- Health is not just the absence of disease but a state of physical, psychological and social well-being.
- Stress can be related to lifestyle.
- Stress can also indirectly affect health such as when it leads to accidents.
- The type, meaning and significance of a disease will affect the degree of stress it causes in a person.
- Various medical conditions are associated with stress.
- Stress affects a whole range of bodily functions, but especially the immune system.

CHAPTER 5

The stress scoreboard

SPECIFIC PSYCHOLOGICAL DISORDERS OR PROBLEMS

LET'S just briefly consider a few specific psychological disorders and some problems that are commonly associated with high stress levels. To make this clear, we begin by dividing the stress response into physical reactions, psychological reactions and behavioural reactions. As anxiety and depression are two of the most common responses to inordinate stress levels, they are used to illustrate the point. A combination of stress and anxiety or depression can be an extremely debilitating experience.

Anxiety

Anxiety is a unique mix of subjective and physiological events that result in apprehension, tension or uneasiness from anticipation of danger – the source of which is not always known or recognised. It becomes problematical when it interferes with effectiveness in living and emotional comfort. Any situation that is perceived as threatening can evoke an anxiety state, the general symptoms of which are listed in Table 5.1. The intensity and/or duration of such an anxiety state is usually in proportion to the amount or degree of the threat perceived and its time span.

Your perception and the thoughts this conjures up, as well as your previous experience of similar situations, can contribute to your anxiety reaction. However, anxiety is part of everyday life. We experience it when we write exams, when we cross a busy road, drive in heavy traffic, or sometimes even when we go shopping. So, like with stress, the aim is not to eradicate anxiety, but to overcome an excessive and debilitating level which may lead to anxiety disorders, among other things. It isn't healthy to become over-stressed because of some stress in your life, nor should you become over anxious about being slightly anxious. You should try to remember the normality of positive stress, and the normality of normal anxiety if you experience it.

Although anxiety has probably always been experienced to some degree, Freud coined the term 'anxiety neurosis'. He contributed significantly to our understanding of anxiety and emphasised that it

42

can act as a warning, signalling a need for a change in our lives. Freud also distinguished between threats in the external world and those coming from the internal world (from within the person). For him, outside threats resulted in objective anxiety whereas internally caused anxiety he called neurotic anxiety. He recognised, though, that objective anxiety resulting from outside threats can sometimes lead to neurotic anxiety. It is interesting to note that Freud himself is said to have suffered from a 'poor house neurosis', seen in the society in which he lived in Austria. He grew up in a typical middle class society in Vienna, and expressed anxiety about not earning enough to keep up with the social expectations of the time.

Not only is anxiety a common experience, it is also a common response to stress and it can, in itself, cause further stress. Being both a cause and symptom of stress, it can create a vicious stress cycle from which it is difficult to escape unless you change your perception of the scenarios that produce it and alter the thoughts that perpetuate it.

Because anxiety can have a useful function, it is important to distinguish between normal and pathological anxiety and to remember that anxiety itself can also be a component of many medical and other psychological disorders. It can sometimes be to your advantage to respond to normal anxiety in certain threatening situations. For example, when you are driving a car and you are trying to avoid an accident, you might experience a certain amount of normal anxiety. Thus, a measure of normal anxiety is commonly experienced by most people. At the other extreme, if you are exposed to a severely traumatic incident like a car-hijacking or assault or serious accident, you could develop abnormal anxiety such as experienced in a post-traumatic stress disorder, in which flashbacks (involuntary occurrences of perceptual disturbances and/or feelings of re-experiencing the event) and various other stress-related symptoms can occur. Post-traumatic stress disorder usually involves psychological stress of a magnitude that would be traumatic for virtually everyone, and as the term implies, it develops after the trauma. Although stress is a primary cause in the development of post-traumatic stress disorder, it is not the only factor to be considered. Individual pre-existing physical and psychological factors, as well as events after the trauma, are also important. Inadequate psychosocial support systems can play a particularly important role, along with other factors.

Normal anxiety must also be distinguished from fear. Fear is a response to a known, external definite threat, whereas anxiety is more diffuse. Fear in itself can, however, also cause anxiety, such as in fear of being hijacked again. When normal anxiety is simply an alerting signal to warn you to react, it can have an adaptive function, such as avoiding

TABLE 5.1

GENERAL SYMPTOMS OF ANXIETY	
THE PHYSICAL REACTIONS CAN INCLUDE:	
✓ DYSPNEA/SHORTNESS OF BREATH	✓ TREMBLING/SHAKING
✓ PALPITATIONS/TACHYCARDIA/ FAST HEARTBEAT	✓ DIZZINESS/LIGHTHEADEDNESS/ WANTING TO FAINT/PASS OUT
✓ EXCESSIVE PERSPIRATION	✓ FEELINGS OF CHOKING/ SMOTHERING
✓ NAUSEA/BUTTERFLIES IN THE STOMACH	✓ ABDOMINAL DISTRESS
✓ PARESTHESIAS/NUMBNESS OR TINGLING SENSATIONS	✓ TROUBLE IN SWALLOWING/ FEELING OF HAVING A LUMP IN THE THROAT
✓ HOT FLUSHES	✓ CHILLS
✓ CHEST DISCOMFORT/PAIN	✓ TENSION PAIN/HEADACHES
✓ MUSCLE TENSION	✓ FREQUENT URINATION
✓ CLAMMY HANDS	✓ A DRY MOUTH
THE PSYCHOLOGICAL REACTIONS CAN INCLUDE:	
✓ FEAR OF LOSING YOUR MIND/ LOSING CONTROL	✓ FEELING THAT YOU WILL MAKE A FOOL OF YOURSELF
✓ DEPERSONALISATION/ DEREALISATION	✓ AVOIDING PEOPLE
✓ FEELING KEYED UP/ON EDGE	✓ FEELING IRRITABLE
✓ THINKING THAT YOU CAN'T GET AWAY FROM PROBLEMS	✓ THINKING THAT ON ENTERING A ROOM FULL OF PEOPLE EVERY ONE IN THE ROOM IS LOOKING AT YOU
THE BEHAVIOURAL REACTIONS CAN INCLUDE:	
✓ BECOMING SNAPPY AND ARGUMENTATIVE	✓ RUSHING AROUND
✓ FEELING RESTRICTED IN SOCIAL ACTIVITIES AND HOBBIES	✓ EASY FATIGUEABILITY/ALWAYS FEELING TIRED AND NOT KNOWING WHY
✓ DEVELOPING VIGILANCE IN SCANNING (YOU'RE ALWAYS ON THE LOOK OUT TO SEE WHAT IS GOING TO HIT YOU NEXT)	✓ EXCESSIVE WORRY/ APPREHENSIVE ANTICIPATION OF FUTURE DANGER OR MISFORTUNE
✓ EXAGGERATED STARTLE RESPONSE/TENDING TO OVER-REACT	✓ DRINKING MORE ALCOHOL OR INCREASING SMOKING HABITS OR MEDICINE INTAKE
✓ RESTLESSNESS	✓ FIDGETING
✓ CONCENTRATION PROBLEMS	✓ DISTURBED EATING/SLEEPING PATTERN

a car accident, or taking precautions against hijacking when driving in high-risk areas. Sometimes anxiety may also be accompanied by feverish activity to cope and an apprehensive anticipation of future danger or misfortune. This can, of course, be highly stressful.

DIFFERENT SUB-TYPES OF ANXIETY DISORDERS

There are various sub-types of anxiety disorders. According to the American Psychiatric Association these can be divided into:

* panic disorder with or without agoraphobia (fear of being in places or situations that would make escape difficult or embarrassing, or that help may not be available in case a panic attack occurs);
* specific and social phobias (a phobia is an irrational fear);
* obsessive-compulsive disorder (which consists of repetitive, intentional or stereo-typed thoughts or acts such as thinking that you might hurt somebody in a traffic accident and constantly checking whether this is so);
* post-traumatic stress disorder;
* acute stress disorder;
* generalised anxiety disorder (continuous, excessive worry and apprehensive expectations about possible misfortunes or ill health that are difficult to control);
* anxiety due to a specific medical condition;
* substance-induced anxiety; and
* adjustment disorder with anxiety (anxiety caused by a specific event which is difficult to adjust to, such as a change at school, work or home).

Panic attacks, acute stress, and post-traumatic stress have almost become stock phrases in today's world, and have been common topics of conversations and magazine articles. The term 'panic' is derived from Greek mythology. According to the story, the cloven-footed and dwarfish Greek god Pan was lonely and moody. He played practical jokes by unexpectedly jumping out of a cave with a terrifying scream when a wanderer passed by. The fright and acute terror this caused the 'victim' came to be known as 'panic'.

Today, a panic attack is considered to be a discreet period of sudden intense apprehension, fear, discomfort or terror associated with feelings of impending doom, an urge to escape and various other symptoms. These can include the fear of going crazy or losing control, shortness of breath, dizziness, lightheadedness, chest pain, palpitations, and smothering or choking sensations. The person has a feeling that a catastrophe is about to happen. On average the attack lasts between 10 to 20 minutes, but for the person it feels as though it will never end.

Acute stress, on the other hand, occurs immediately following the aftermath of an extremely traumatic experience and has symptoms that are similar to post-traumatic stress, except that they occur within the first month after the trauma. Post-traumatic stress is symptomatic of re-experiencing (flashbacks) an extremely traumatic experience, increased arousal and the avoidance of reminders of the traumatic event. Various other symptoms include: recurrent and intrusive distressing recollections, images, thoughts, or perceptions of the traumatic event (children may express repetitive play with themes of aspects of the trauma); and recurrent distressing dreams of the event (children may have frightening dreams without recognisable content).

Depression

Depression is a condition that has been described since antiquity and is common in today's society. A World Health Organisation survey recently reported that depression (the fourth most serious psychological health threat in 1990) will rise to become the second most serious health threat by the year 2020. We all become sad at one time or another, and feeling down is not necessarily indicative of clinical depression. As with stress and anxiety, sadness is a normal human reaction in life. Sadness, however, is considered to have passed into depression when your depressed mood has become pathological (abnormal), has been observed to persist for too long and is interfering with your normal functioning. A combination of intensity, severity and duration of the symptoms of depression are important markers in making the diagnosis.

It has been argued that in some cases the depressed person withdraws psychologically from the 'fight' response and the unbearable stress associated with it into a depressed state. The slowing down of such a person's thought processes may also tend to decrease the psychological pain caused by stress, because the quantity of stressful stimuli that has to be processed by thinking about them is reduced. The problem is that any relief from stress by withdrawing into a depression brings about the unpleasant symptoms of the depression itself.

DIFFERENT SUB-TYPES OF DEPRESSION

Depression can be influenced by different factors including biochemical, constitutional and cultural ones, as well as stress. Psychosocial stressors can cause biochemical and other changes in brain function which can play a role in the development of depression, and a variety of such stressors have been identified that precede certain types of depression.

As in the case of anxiety there are different types of depressive disorders (also referred to as mood disorders because they reflect severe disturbances of mood). These disorders vary in symptomatology, and according to the American Psychiatric Association can be divided into:

- major depressive disorder (during which there are one or more major depressive episodes);
- dysthymic disorder (a chronically depressed mood for most of the day that lasts for at least two years);
- biopolar disorder (mood swings that can include manic episodes whereby some people alternate between depression and mania – mania is diagnosed when there are episodes of highly elevated mood, overactivity, irritability, loss of judgement and abnormal euphoria);
- cyclothymic disorder (a milder form of mood swings);
- depression due to a general medical condition;
- substance-induced depression; and
- adjustment disorder with depressed mood (depression caused by a specific stressful event which is difficult to adjust to, such as specific problems at school, work or home).

There is also a condition known as seasonal affective disorder (or SAD for short) which is seen in people who show a seasonal pattern in their depression. Such people tend to become depressed at a particular time in the year, often during winter.

Estimates of the exact incidence and prevalence of depression vary widely, but it seems that in the general population certain depressive disorders occur in up to 15 per cent of adults and that all types of depressive disorders described for adults also occur in children and adolescents. Depression in infancy and childhood is probably more common than previously thought, and earlier reported low prevalence rates appear to be due to inadequate diagnosis rather than to adequate reflections of occurrence. Depression is a major reason for hospitalising patients, and is significantly associated with many medical and surgical problems and with people who suffer from chronic pain, as well as with a variety of other conditions and suicidal behaviour.

Although it can be associated with various causes, stress in particular can play a major role in depression. It has been shown that certain stressful life events are very important in this regard. For example, onset of depression may be a risk factor in an adult who, as a child, lost a parent. Suffering the loss of something (even goals in life) or someone important (a spouse or a loved one) is a common stressful life event associated with depression. There are many studies which point to a relationship between family and/or work problems and depression. It is also common to find a sense of learned helplessness in some depressed people. Such learned helplessness can develop when these people's perceptions result in feelings of loss of control and mastery over their own lives and their environment, so that they get trapped in a cycle of engaging in persistent misperceptions, misinterpretations and negative thoughts. If unchecked, this leads to further sense of helplessness and could eventually result in feelings of hopelessness and suicidal thoughts. In fact, this sort of depression has been described as 'a belief in one's own helplessness'.

Some of the more general symptoms of depression are mentioned in Table 5.2.

Suicidal behaviour

Stress is a major risk factor in suicidal behaviour. Domestic stress, especially that stemming from family problems, is important in this regard. A recent study by myself and a colleague confirmed previous research showing a clear relationship between early parental loss and later onset of depression and suicidal behaviour in young adults. We found that the loss of parents through bereavement or divorce represented an unpleasant episode or trauma in young children's lives, and if the stress was not dealt with adequately, then they could end up suffering significant disruptions later in life. In some cases this unresolved stress escalated into psychological disorders such as anxiety disorders (especially panic disorder) or even into suicidal behaviour. The implications of this research are clear: if children are exposed to severe stress and it is not adequately resolved, the consequences can be far-reaching in adulthood – even fatal.

Another risk factor is a feeling of hopelessness coupled with depression which could result in suicidal thoughts and behaviour.

TABLE 5.2

GENERAL SYMPTOMS OF DEPRESSION	
THE PHYSICAL REACTIONS CAN INCLUDE:	
✓ LETHARGY/TIREDNESS/LACK OF ENERGY	✓ SEXUAL DISTURBANCES
✓ PSYCHOMOTOR RETARDATION/ SENSE OF BEING PHYSICALLY SLOWED DOWN	✓ PSYCHOMOTOR AGITATION/A SENSE OF BEING PHYSICALLY AGITATED
✓ SIGNIFICANT WEIGHT LOSS (A REDUCTION OF MORE THAN FIVE PER CENT OF BODY MASS IN ONE MONTH WITHOUT BEING ON DIET)	✓ DIFFICULTY IN GETTING THE DAY STARTED
✓ POOR DIGESTION/ CONSTIPATION	✓ VAGUE ACHES/PAINS/GENERAL MALAISE
THE PSYCHOLOGICAL REACTIONS CAN INCLUDE:	
✓ THOUGHTS OF WORTHLESSNESS/ BEING A FAILURE	✓ THOUGHTS THAT THE FUTURE IS BLEAK/HOPELESS
✓ THOUGHTS THAT ALL YOUR EFFORTS ARE USELESS	✓ LOSS OF INTEREST IN PLEASURE OR MOST ACTIVITIES/NOTHING IS FUN ANYMORE
✓ THOUGHTS THAT YOU ARE USELESS	✓ THOUGHTS THAT IT IS ALWAYS YOUR FAULT IF THINGS GO WRONG
✓ FEELING SORRY FOR YOURSELF	✓ PERCEIVING EVERYTHING IN THE WORST WAY
✓ FEELINGS OF EMPTINESS	✓ THOUGHTS THAT LIFE IS NOT WORTH LIVING/SUICIDAL THOUGHTS
✓ FREQUENT/PERSISTENT DEPRESSED MOOD	✓ EXCESSIVE/INAPPROPRIATE GUILT
THE BEHAVIOURAL REACTIONS CAN INCLUDE:	
✓ DIMINISHED CONCENTRATION	✓ INDECISIVENESS
✓ CRYING A LOT/OFTEN LOOKING DOWNCAST	✓ BEING IDLE FOR PROLONGED PERIODS
✓ STARTING THINGS BUT NOT FINISHING THEM	✓ GIVING UP HOBBIES/SPORT/ SOCIAL ACTIVITIES
✓ EATING DISTURBANCES/POOR APPETITE/EXCESSIVE APPETITE	✓ SLEEP DISTURBANCES/INSOMNIA (SLEEPING TOO LITTLE)/ HYPERSOMNIA (SLEEPING TOO MUCH)
✓ SPENDING TOO MUCH TIME ALONE	✓ NEGLECTING YOUR PHYSICAL APPEARANCE
✓ FORGETFULNESS	✓ DRINKING MORE ALCOHOL OR INCREASING SMOKING HABITS OR MEDICINE INTAKE
✓ IRRITABILITY/SNAPPINESS	✓ DOING THINGS MORE SLOWLY THAN BEFORE

Hopelessness can develop as a result of continuous negative expectations of the future. This is in a large measure affected by a person's perceptions and thoughts about the future. Suicidal behaviour in modern society is almost endemic in some communities. It has many faces, and what sometimes appears to be something else (an accident, for example), could in fact be suicidal behaviour.

It is not always so much the thought of wanting to die, but rather of wanting to escape the psychological pain caused by depression and stress that leads a person towards eventual suicidal behaviour. Suicidal behaviour is not a psychological disorder in itself but must be viewed as a symptom of something deeper. Although it can be associated with stress, it can also be the result of other factors such as, for example, depression or another psychological disorder.

DIFFERENT SUB-TYPES OF SUICIDAL BEHAVIOUR

Some of the sub-types of suicidal behaviour include not only actual suicide or attempted suicide (a fortuitous survival of a suicide), but also:

- parasuicide (a non-lethal suicide-like act with low intent usually performed to focus attention on the person's problems);
- in some cases family murder, which could be a form of extended suicide (where the head of the family kills other family members before deciding to commit suicide); and
- indirect suicide (where the person leaves the decision of whether the suicidal behaviour will be successful to fate, as seen in people who literally play Russian Roulette with their lives). Another example of the latter is driving so recklessly as to invite an accident in the hope that the driver won't survive it.

Such various types of suicidal behaviours are commonly associated with depression, helplessness, hopelessness and high stress levels.

Adjustment disorders

Most people, even so-called stable personalities, will break down if the going gets tough enough or when conditions of overwhelming stress occur. Some may develop transient (temporary) psychological problems such as adjustment disorders (American Psychiatric Association). When this occurs, the person shows a short-term, maladaptive (unhealthy) response to stress. It is frequently evident in physical disease, social and/or occupational or academic impairment. Factors that are important in this regard include the nature of the stress, how the person perceives the stress and how vulnerable they are to such stress. Essentially the person has difficulty adjusting to change, and the causative stressor can be clearly identified.

People who are inflexible and find change frightening, are more likely to develop difficulties in adjusting from what they perceive to be negative stress – whether the stressors are single, multiple or recurrent. Although the severity of the stressor is also influenced by its duration, timing and context in the person's life, the negative reaction is not absolutely predictable by its severity – that is, different people could react differently to the same level of severity of stress. Adjustment disorders can be associated with anxiety and depression as we saw earlier, or with a mixture of both, or with disturbed conduct, or with a mixed disturbance of emotions and behaviour. They can also be general and unspecified.

Dissociative disorders

Dissociative disorders are a group of disorders in which there is an alteration of consciousness, identity, perception of the environment or motor behaviour. Some part or more of these functions are lost. Psychologically healthy people have a consolidated sense of self, but in dissociative disorders this is disturbed. In essence such people escape from their core personalities with their painful connotations. This arises as a defence against an extremely stressful trauma, in order to help them to escape from the trauma at the time that it happens and to delay working through the implications of the trauma. Memory loss is a common aspect of dissociative disorders, and this can include the inability to remember important personal information of an extremely stressful nature (dissociative amnesia). Sometimes people even forget their own personal identity, or can't recall their past, such as in a disorder known as dissociative fugue.

DIFFERENT SUB-TYPES OF DISSOCIATIVE DISORDERS

According to the American Psychiatric Association, in addition to dissociative amnesia and dissociative fugue, other dissociative disorders include:

- dissociative identity disorder (multiple personality disorder), where there is a presence of two or more identities or personalities in the same person that recurrently control that person's behaviour;
- depersonalisation disorder, where the person repeatedly experiences feelings of being detached from the self – almost as if that person becomes an observer from the outside or feels like they are living in a dream;
- derealisation, which involves a feeling of detachment from one's environment;
- dissociative trance disorder, where the person is in a trance state which is not part of a normal, accepted cultural or religious practice;
- Ganser syndrome, which involves the voluntary production of severe psychological/psychiatric symptoms and providing approximate answers to questions or continuously talking past the point (for example, if asked how many wheels there are in a car, the person answers seven); and
- certain dissociative states in people who have been the victims of intensive and prolonged coercive persuasion, such as found in brainwashing, indoctrination or thought reform.

Sleep disorders

Stress is closely associated with sleep disturbances. One of the earliest symptoms of stress can in fact be disruption of sleep. Undue stress can be associated with circulation of high levels of certain hormones in the body, as discussed in the function of the endocrine system. This produces an aroused state and can interfere with sleep. Sleep disturbances may also be related to several other psychological conditions (especially anxiety and depression), as well as to various physical diseases. They can also occur because of problems with the sleep–wake schedule (disturbances of the circadian rhythm or body clock as in shift work or international flights). Sleep can also be complicated by a number of medications and other substances such as alcohol and drinks or food that contain caffeine (which can induce multiple awakenings and reduce sleep efficiency). Medication-induced causes of stress and other psychological disorders have come under the searchlight recently because of their increasingly common occurrence.

The function of sleep is primarily restorative, and is crucial for normal thermoregulation (regulation of the body's temperature) and conservation of energy. Up to one third of the population suffers from occasional sleep disturbances during their lifetime, of which insomnia is the most common (apparently more so in women than in men). The prevalence of insomnia increases with age. In addition, there are different kinds of sleep disorders, mostly characterised by insomnia, hypersomnia (excessive amounts of sleep), parasomnia (nightmares, sleep terrors, sleep walking) and sleep–wake schedule disturbances.

Sleep also plays an important role in the response to stress as many of the adverse effects of sleep disturbances are closely linked to emotional and physical recovery, and sleep disturbances can be a symptom of stress as well as being stressful in itself. For example, sleep or sleep deprivation can lead to psychological distress and, if prolonged, can even result in hallucinations and delusions. The effects of sleep disturbances are therefore self-perpetuating and significantly diminish our resistance to stress.

STAGES OF SLEEP

Sleep is associated with various physiological changes including respiration, cardiac function, muscle tone, temperature, the secretion of hormones, blood pressure and brain waves. In life there are various rhythms that you are exposed to, the most obvious one being the circadian rhythm which governs the differences between wakefulness and sleeping. Likewise, your sleep is not a continuous state because of its ultradian rhythm. Sleep consists of two alternating states: non-rapid eye movement (non-REM) and rapid eye movement (REM) sleep.

During sleep two types of waves occur, alpha and delta waves. Most physiological functions are slower during non-REM sleep, which is a peaceful state. When you close your eyes and attempt to sleep, your brain produces alpha waves at a low-frequency rhythm of about eight to twelve cycles per second. These alpha waves are associated with you being in a relaxed state and not concentrating on anything specific. They gradually slow down further until you fall asleep. Eventually delta waves are produced by your brain. These are very slow waves of about one to three cycles per second. You are now in deep sleep. During this process of drifting into sleep you go through four stages, each one deeper than the next:

- Stage one occurs when you drift on the edge of consciousness in a state of light sleep and if awakened you may recall a few visual images or fantasies;
- Stage two occurs when light sounds or minor noises are unlikely to disturb you;

- Stage three occurs when your breathing and pulse slow down, your temperature drops and your muscles relax, delta waves are present and it is difficult to arouse you;
- Stage four occurs when the delta waves have taken over and you are in deep sleep. Although it might sound like a contradiction in terms, this last stage is the stage during which sleep walking or talking occur.

Each of these four stages is accompanied by different brain waves. The entire sequence takes about 35 to 45 minutes and then reverses itself back to stage one which you reach about 70 to 90 minutes after sleep first commenced.

However at this point, stage one does not revert to drowsy wakefulness, but your brain starts to emit long bursts of irregular waves and certain physiological changes occur such as convulsive twitches in your face or fingers, an erect penis (if you are a male because vascular tissue relaxes and blood fills the genital area and not because you have sexual dreams), engorgement of the vaginal walls and lubrication (if you are a woman), skeletal muscles that go limp, etc. You are now supposed to be in a 'light' sleep but it is hard to wake up. You have actually gone into REM sleep. In REM sleep, brain oxygen increases and you show brainwave patterns almost akin to the waking state. Your body is relaxed but your brain is active which is why REM sleep has also been called 'paradoxical' sleep. The more eventful your dreams, the more frequent and rapid your eye movements become. REM periods occur about every 90 minutes in adults, about four to six times a night and make up about one fifth to a quarter of the total sleep time. REM and non-REM sleep alternate throughout the night. The majority of REM sleep is associated with dreaming. Although dreams occur during non-REM sleep, they tend to be less vivid.

This book deals with the role of perceptions, thoughts, emotions and behaviour in managing stress. These functions are mostly explained as part of your wakeful, conscious state when you are alert and you focus on external and/or internal changes and events or stressors. However, part of your mind consists of your subconscious mind, which can also affect your responses. Subconscious awareness can be brought into conscious awareness when necessary. Likewise, there are other states that you could find yourself in, such as dreaming when you are asleep or day dreaming when you are awake. There are also other types of awareness which include altered states of consciousness like hypnotic states, when your level of consciousness is altered by certain drugs, and certain forms of dissociation where consciousness is separated into different parts associated with specific psychological disorders as discussed earlier.

DREAMS

Dreams open up fascinating worlds during which your focus is inward. When you have gone to sleep, the theatre of your life becomes the theatre of your dreams in which you replay aspects of your life experiences and in which reality and reason are no longer the dominant forces. Sometimes you might remember your dreams, and other times not. You forget dreams for various reasons including the fact that they might not be worth remembering. It is also thought that there might be a memory shut down when you sleep, because memory is one of the brain functions that rests during sleep. Sometimes people say one cannot dream in colour. This is a myth. What is more likely is that the memory of the colours might be forgotten more easily than the actual dream. While you are dreaming, the dream might be vivid, terrifying or peaceful but when you wake up your dream might be recalled as bizarre, illogical or even frightening. Various problems such as nightmares, waking-up in a panic-stricken state of anxiety or night terrors, can be linked to stress.

It is interesting to compare day dreaming with sleep dreaming. In both your focus is inward, but day dreams tend to be more about immediate every day things which you might wonder or fantasise about. Most people day dream – the rhythm of which can be affected by the situation they are in. It often occurs when they are alone or involved in routine activities. Day dreams can interfere with concentration, but psychologists who have researched this area point out that they are normal and can sometimes even be good for you because they can provide a positive spin off for escape from the stress of reality.

Sexual disorders

In couples, a well-balanced, harmonious and loving sex life can be important for general health, and can influence the ability to manage stress as well. Conversely, the lack of a harmonious sexual relationship in couples can lead to stress and increase low self-esteem and loss of self-confidence. Sexual response can, amongst other things, be disrupted by stress or its consequences, especially where stress is associated with other psychological disorders or substance abuse. Alcohol abuse is a well-known culprit in this regard.

There are several sub-types of sexual dysfunctions (American Psychiatric Association). These include sexual desire disorders, sexual arousal disorders, orgasmic disorders, sexual pain disorders and sexual dysfunctions due to medical problems. They must be distinguished from the sexual paraphilias which the person in the street sometimes refers to as perversions, such as exhibitionism, fetishism, voyeurism, etc. Although sexual problems can be caused by other factors (including medical ones), many can be related to stress. Some of these problems can also become a stressor in themselves (such as premature ejaculation or difficulty in achieving or sustaining an erection).

Stress has also been linked with infertility in some instances. It works both ways. For example, if a couple cannot have a child, it can be experienced as stressful, and stress itself can affect hormone production. Further, a link has been discovered between stress and the male hormone testosterone. Testosterone production can be reduced by prolonged stress and a testosterone deficiency can be associated with a host of both emotional and physical problems (including premature aging of the heart and the circulatory system). In addition, lack of hormone production in males can produce similar symptoms to what females suffer during menopause, including depression, fatigue and lack of drive – especially sex drive. The sex hormones are associated with the endocrine system, which, in turn, is linked to the stress response as we saw in Chapter 2. So, being stressed may have an impact on hormone levels. These in turn may upset sexual behaviour such as arousal, erection and orgasm.

It is helpful to consider the various sexual dysfunctions against a background of the normal sexual response cycle. The normal human sexual response cycle can be described in terms of four phases, based on the well-known work of William Masters and Virgina Johnson (Figure 5.1).

The first phase of desire, excitement or 'build-up' results from sexual stimulation which may be physical or psychological or from a combination of both. It frequently starts in the mind, the person (especially males) are 'turned on' by something erotic (in reality or fantasy). This mental change triggers nerve impulses through the body prompting various physical changes, and can result from direct stimulation (touching, stroking, kissing, etc.), or indirect stimulation

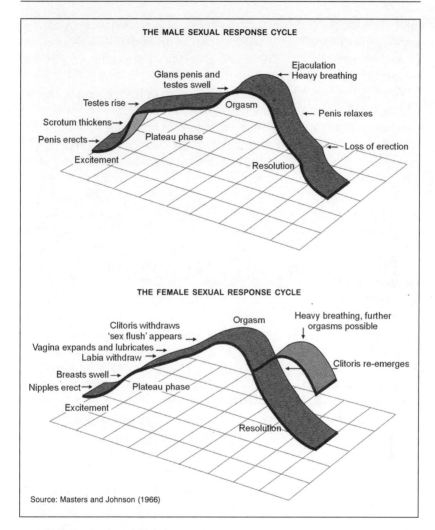

THE MALE SEXUAL RESPONSE CYCLE

THE FEMALE SEXUAL RESPONSE CYCLE

Source: Masters and Johnson (1966)

FIGURE 5.1 *The normal sexual response cycle.*

(vision, smell, emotions, thoughts, etc.). A subjective sense of sexual pleasure accompanies the physiological changes.

The second or plateau phase is attained if stimulation is continued, and it involves a levelling off of sexual tensions. It can vary in duration according to the requirements for the next phase, which is the orgasmic phase.

The third or orgasmic phase, which is the shortest phase of the human sexual response cycle, typically involves a total body response and a sudden discharge of accumulated sexual tension (it results in maximum excitement). Reactions vary widely depending on personality, experience and various other factors, and no two women experience orgasms exactly in the same way. A great deal of stress can be caused by unrealistic expectations and lack of understanding in this regard.

The final or resolution phase follows the orgasmic phase, during which the body returns to its original unaroused state, and is accompanied by a sense of general relaxation, well-being and muscular relaxation. Following the completion of the cycle, most men generally experience physical difficulty with further erection and orgasm for a period, though healthier men are arousable sooner and the sexual response cycle (from excitement to ejaculation) can be achieved quicker than in unhealthier men. In contrast, most women may be able to respond again almost immediately and some may be able to have another orgasm very soon, referred to as multiple orgasms.

There may be inhibitions in the human sexual response cycle at any one or more of these phases, sometimes leading to sexual dysfunction. Couples' health status, their general lifestyles, and the state of their relationship can influence their sexual response and cause sexual dysfunction. In particular, sexual function at any of these phases can be adversely affected by stress. Sexual problems may be lifelong or acquired and may be general or situational – for example, limited to a specific partner or to a certain stressful situation. Further, sex crimes, such as rape and sexual violence, can contribute to severe stress-laden responses in victims which can have a profound effect on future sexual activities and relationships.

Somatoform disorders

'Somatic' means 'of the body'. Somatoform disorders, therefore, consist of certain disorders that include physical symptoms such as pain, nausea, etc. for which there are no appropriate medical explanations. The physical symptoms are serious enough to cause significant psychological distress and interference with normal function. There are several of these disorders. According to the American Psychiatric Association, they include:

- somatisation disorder, in which the person displays a host of physical complaints involving many organ systems in the body during which stress and psychological pain are converted into physical symptoms. In a sense, somatisation is a defence mechanism to deal with emotional conflicts and stress, that has been recognised as a disorder since ancient Egypt and an early name for it being hysteria.

- conversion disorder, in which the person converts stress into symptoms that suggest a neurological or other medical condition such as paralysis or blindness;
- hypochondriasis, wherein the person inaccurately interprets physical symptoms and develops a preoccupation with fear of getting a disease – even if there are no grounds for it, this can lead to significant distress and impairment of function in the person;
- body dysmorphic disorder, in which a person has a preoccupation with an imagined defect in appearance such as the shape of the chin, ears, etc.; and
- pain disorder, in which the person complains of pain which cannot fully be explained by a medical condition.

Pain is probably one of the most common general complaints. Stress plays a major role in causing and/or contributing to a variety of factors associated with backaches, headaches and other pain. These problems frequently include a psychosomatic component usually related to prolonged stress, feelings of helplessness and of not knowing how to cope with the stress or its causes. Psychological stress can be made worse by bio-ecological stressors including pollution, poor working conditions and noise. The cost of backaches, headaches and pain in its various forms in Western countries is astounding. Pain is one of the most common causes of time lost from work. This is often made worse when people with such pain don't follow a healthy diet or suitable exercise routine, thus worsening an already unhealthy lifestyle which further leads to more stress, more pain and the perceived need for more medication.

Psychologists have discovered that a person's psychological state can influence the perception of pain. This explains why one person would find a specific pain such as a backache excruciating and another not. Effective psychological interventions in pain would then aim to change a person's perception of discomfort and ability to control emotional and psychological responses. Furthermore, psychic pain (deep sadness, and pain of the heart, mind and spirit) can be as powerful an experience as physical pain, and the suppression of this pain can actually make some physical disorders worse or even lead to certain physical problems. Very often psychic pain is the price some people pay for engaging in relationships, because within every relationship lies the potential for separation or loss.

Typically, most patients in my own research on the abuse of painkillers claim to abuse analgesics because of persistent pain, but especially headaches of varying descriptions, often mentioning migraine (although the symptoms described by them are not always characteristic). They frequently describe their headaches as tension or heaviness of the head. In these patients, headaches are frequently also a side-effect of analgesic, caffeine and other substance abuse, or are caused by withdrawal from such substances. Further, psychogenic (caused by psychological factors) headaches form the basis of one of the most common general medical complaints used to explain away work absenteeism, and are often used to defend lack of engagement in undesired activities, and are prominent symptoms in many psychological disorders including anxiety, depression and sleep disturbances.

HEADACHES

Although prevalence rates may vary, about 80 per cent of the general population per annum suffer from headaches and about 10 to 20 per cent present to physicians with headaches as their primary complaint. Headaches are also common complaints of hypochondriacs, who often seek numerous analgesic prescriptions as a result of their abnormal illness behaviour. Clearly, headaches can also be perceived as a subjective symptom of some other underlying disorder. Stress can exacerbate headaches and back pain irrespective of the underlying causes. In particular the relationship between stress and analgesic and other substance abuse, leading to other disorders where headaches and back pain form part of the symptom complex, needs to be considered in stress management. Generally, of the headaches patients complain about, tension headaches and vascular or migraine headaches with their many variants are quite common, along with psychogenic, cluster and recurring or chronic headaches. It is possible for some patients to present with two types of headaches, such as migraine and tension headaches which can occur simultaneously.

Factitious disorders

In factitious disorders there is an intentional production and misrepresentation of psychological or physical symptoms in order to assume a sick role or to be a patient (American Psychiatric Association). Often such people have a history of stress associated with them perceiving that they have been rejected by their parents with whom they could not form close relationships. They can have strong needs of dependence. The symptoms they feign or misinterpret can be either predominantly psychological or predominantly physical or a combination of both. The psychological symptoms almost resemble a kind of pseudomalingering, and the physical ones are sometimes described as Münchausen syndrome (named after Baron von Münchausen, who wrote many stories about his (mis)adventures in the 18th century). Another example includes pseudologia fantastica (pathological lying with an obsessive tendency to embroider on the truth or lie in a vague and excessive way), where people give limited facts which are mixed with excessive fantasies. Patients, for example, often give false accounts about their lives, such as saying old injuries were sustained in a war when in fact they were never in any war. Or a patient may bring a urine sample to the clinic for testing contaminated by adding things to it rather than having produced it normally.

Substance-related disorders
The widespread legal and illegal abuse of psychoactive (brain-altering) substances (drugs) has many implications for society. A disturbing number of people turn to various substances to deal with stress-related conditions. There is nothing wrong in taking pain killers for pain, enjoying an occasional glass of wine, eating chocolate or drinking a cup of coffee. But, when these and other substances are abused, a problem arises resulting in various substance-related disorders (American Psychiatric Association). This is the concern here. Many of the substances used excessively for stress relief actually make the situation worse, and some provide only palliative relief or transitory soothing. Although appropriate medication can play an important role in the treatment of certain stress-related psychological disorders, stress management that is largely based on taking medication alone, generally has very limited results. Substance-related disorders can have complex causes, but the psychological ones are often related to stress, especially when people engage in inappropriate self-medication to cope with stress. These disorders consist of various sub-types related to the particular substances being taken. They usually result when a person takes a particular substance or substances in an abusive pattern that can also involve physical dependence and/or psychological dependence.

Substance abuse can also result in medical problems or disorders, thereby making the stress much worse. My own studies have shown that the abuse of over-the-counter analgesics (painkillers) commonly starts with stress-related problems (including psychological pain and/or psychological distress for which people incorrectly take painkillers). This can set off a vicious cycle in that, if they abuse certain painkillers for long enough and in large enough quantities, it can lead to serious disease such as end-stage kidney disease and disturbances in brain function. Such people typically either purchase their painkillers over the counter or engage in substance-seeking behaviour by doctor shopping or pharmacy hopping. Generally a cumulative dose of painkillers of four to six tablets or powders daily are ingested, building up to two or more kilograms of painkillers over two or more years. If such quantities are taken it can result in the development of analgesic-related kidney disease or other serious diseases. My research found that, in some cases, patients took doses as high as 10 daily tablets or powders resulting in eventually taking 4 to 11 kilograms of analgesics over a 4 to 10 year period. Painkillers are commonly used as drugs of choice in suicidal behaviour involving overdose. My studies on suicidal behaviour showed that self-poisoning with painkillers and other drugs was by far one of the most prevalent methods used by both adolescents and adults, and accounted for over 90 per cent of suicidal patients seen. This research also showed that although a wide variety of substances were used when overdoses were taken, non-prescription medicines tended to predominate: 25 per cent of adults and 27 per cent of adolescents ingested painkillers when they attempted overdoses. It is interesting to note that according to the same research, psychiatric drugs (available only on prescription) were used by 25 per cent of adults and about 14 per cent of adolescents who attempted overdoses.

Certain substances contained in food (such as caffeine) can trigger or mimic the stress response (that is, their effects can be sympathomimetic). Caffeine is probably one of the most widely used psychoactive substances. Just think of coffee and how much of it is consumed. A cup of coffee usually contains between 100 and 150 mg of caffeine, and a cup of tea about one third as much. Caffeine is also found in many over-the-counter medicines and in a great variety of foods and beverages, such as cocoa, chocolate and soft drinks. The time it takes to metabolise (chemically process in the body) half of caffeine (its 'half-life') is about 3 to 10 hours and the time to peak concentration in the blood is about 30 to 60 minutes. Caffeine easily crosses the barrier that separates the blood from the brain (the blood–brain barrier which prevents certain substances in the blood from entering the cerebrospinal fluid). Doses of about 100 mg can induce a mild euphoria, but when doses exceed 300 mg they can be associated with increased anxiety and an unpleasant mood. Tolerance and withdrawal symptoms can occur after excessive use of caffeine. In people who abuse caffeine, caffeine-related disorders have been described. Common symptoms include restlessness, nervousness, excitement, sleep disturbances, irritability, agitation, anxiety, muscle twitching, flushed face, nausea, diuresis (increased urine production), sleep disturbances, gastro-intestinal disturbances and excessive perspiration. Large doses (one gram or more) can cause rambling speech, confused thinking, cardiac arrhythmias, marked agitation and even visual hallucinations. The quick consumption of 10 g or more can cause seizures, respiratory failures and even death.

DRUGS AND CO-MORBIDITY

Substance dependence can include: physiological dependence (evidence of tolerance which occurs when you need more of the same substance, or withdrawal which occurs when you experience high levels of distress because of a reduction in or cessation of using the substance); taking increasingly larger amounts with unsuccessful attempts at cutting down on intake; impaired social, occupational and recreational activities; and continued use despite knowing that recurrent physical or psychological problems are caused by taking the substance.

On the other hand, substance abuse occurs when substance dependence is not yet present, but the abuse interferes with fulfilling major work, school, study and/or social obligations or roles. Often a pattern of repeated use of substances occurs despite the person engaging in physically hazardous situations such as driving a car, or when there are repeated substance-related legal problems, or even when the abuser knows it results in recurrent social, interpersonal and work problems.

In substance dependence or abuse, co-morbidity is frequently present. That is, the person can develop two or more psychological disorders simultaneously. For example, stress, substance abuse, depression and suicidal behaviour in the same person are common. Likewise, simultaneous dependence on or abuse of more than one substance can occur (polysubstance abuse). That is, the person regularly uses two or more substances, such as tranquillisers, alcohol and cigarettes at the same time . This is not uncommon, as many people who abuse one substance also tend to use others excessively. For example, the smoker who drinks might smoke more under the influence of alcohol, and because of the after-effects might have an increased need for coffee or pain-killers to cope with the discomfort.

Another one of the more common substances people turn to in order to cope with stress, is alcohol. Certain medicines and psychiatric drugs can make the effects of alcohol worse. There are serious risks in combining such medicines and alcohol as their effects co-operate or work together (that is, they are synergistic). Apart from the well-known effects of alcohol on the brain, behaviour and psychological functioning, its abuse can also lead to many medical complications. Almost every organ in the body can be adversely affected by alcohol abuse. Problems can include new psychological impairment (brain damage) and many others, including predisposing a person to infections because of immune suppression, cirrhosis of the liver, hypertension, sexual problems, gastrointestinal problems, various drug interactions and sleep disturbances, apart from the obvious behavioural effects seen in a person under the influence of alcohol. The abuse of alcohol is also associated with a host of social and work performance problems, behavioural problems, impairment of brain function, depression, a high suicide rate and anxiety disorders. Because it interferes with so many aspects of the person's life, it contributes directly to a progressively weaker ability to combat stress. When it is consumed, the resultant euphoric effects are temporary and hide the fact that alcohol is actually a depressant. Because most people become uninhibited under the influence of alcohol, the wrong impression is created that it is a stimulant. So, despite the short-term lift it causes, it can eventually end up a serious problem if abused. Approximately 10 per cent of alcohol that is consumed is absorbed from the stomach and the remainder from the small intestine. Peak blood concentration occurs within 30 to 90 minutes, depending on whether the alcohol was taken with food or not, as food can delay alcohol absorption. Once alcohol finds its way into the blood stream, it is distributed to all body tissues. Approximately 90 per cent of alcohol is metabolised through oxidation in the liver and the rest is excreted unchanged by the kidneys and the lungs.

Tobacco smoking is often defended by smokers who claim that it helps them cope with stress, despite the fact that the health-risk effects of smoking have been widely published. These aside, what many people don't realise is that there is a negative link between smoking and stress. Smoking is increasingly a more common response to stress, and paradoxically smokers argue that they use smoking in order to relieve tension. Although there might be a temporary psychological effect that the smoker finds calming, physically the effects of the nicotine found in tobacco can mimic the stress response. Like caffeine and alcohol, nicotine can also be a stressor. This is because it stimulates the adrenal glands that release hormones associated with producing the stress response such as an increase in heart rate, respiration rate and blood pressure. Nicotine causes an increase in the circulation of the hormones noradrenaline (norepinephrine) and adrenaline (epinephrine), and the hormones ACTH and cortisol which contribute to the basic stimulatory effect of nicotine. The nicotine contained in even one cigarette can affect the adrenaline levels in the blood. The effect on the stress response becomes compounded if nicotine is taken with caffeine or other substances that trigger the stress response, as their combined effects are also synergistic. If taken regularly with other substances that act as biochemical stressors, it is clear that the effects can become even more profound. Interestingly, reports show that a very high proportion of people with psychological disorders smoke. My own research on the abuse of painkillers and on suicidal behaviour mentioned earlier, confirmed that excessive smoking behaviour was prevalent in many of the patients I studied. Generally, approximately 25 per cent of nicotine inhaled when smoking reaches the blood, and it ends up in the brain within 15 seconds. The half-life of nicotine is about two hours. Nicotine can have short-term stimulatory effects and for some smokers even improves concentration temporarily, but long-term use has been shown to be extremely harmful and the health benefits of not smoking (or giving up if one does) are well documented. Nicotine is a highly toxic substance, and if the same amounts that the average smoker inhales should, for example, be eaten, the health effects could be extremely dangerous over a very short period of time. A recent World Health Organisation report states that in the world every 10 seconds another person dies because of tobacco use. About three million deaths a year in the early 1990s were caused by tobacco use. This figure is steadily increasing. The warning is that if current smoking trends are not reversed, smoking-related deaths are expected to rise to 10 million per year by the 2020s or early 2030s. It is estimated that 70 per cent of those deaths will occur in developing countries as these are the communities that are increasingly targeted by tobacco companies.

Burnout

People sometimes complain of burnout. This is usually associated with overload, which occurs when the demands they are faced with become so excessive that an inordinate stress response is aroused and sustained. They are literally overstimulated and the demands made on them completely exceed their capacity to meet them. Because it is prolonged and inordinate, they exceed their optimal level of functioning and enter a negative phase of stress which leads

to mental and physical fatigue. Burnout can occur in various situations. For example, it is frequently a stress reaction to intense
investment by people of time and energy (time pressures) in work
coupled with chronic, unrelenting emotional pressure, excessive
responsibility, lack of support, excessive expectations from themselves and from others, and the inability to cope. Such prolonged
overload of extreme stress can result in total exhaustion so that
eventually they can no longer function adequately at work or at
home. Burnout can, however, also occur in other spheres of life,
even within the arena of artistic creativity or in writers. Sexual
burnout has also been described and has to do with feelings of
physical depletion, emotional emptiness, a poor self-concept and
sexual helplessness related to the perception that little can be done
to rekindle the erstwhile passion once experienced in a loving
relationship.

People sometimes ask me: 'But how do I know that I am experiencing the symptoms of burnout?' Well, a rule of thumb explanation
would be to perceive stress as a motivating resource that leads you to
perform optimally, so that you can be productive, creative, healthy
and communicative. However, as soon as you get past this level of
optimal performance because your stress becomes too high and too
prolonged, you will start showing signs of poor productivity, inefficiency, low levels of creativity, poorer health, and poorer communication skills with resultant poorer interpersonal relationships.
Instead of dealing with this negative stress, you push yourself more to
achieve the same earlier optimal functioning, possibly even taking all
sorts of substances (including medication) as aids. By doing so, you set
in motion a process that undermines both your psychological and
physical well-being. Eventually, the effects of all-round fatigue form a
vicious cycle that becomes stressful in itself, so that ultimately you are
physically and psychologically exhausted. This gradual decline in
functioning is illustrated in Table 5.3. It's a bit like a car that has been
driven relentlessly with little maintenance that gets driven harder and
harder with less and less maintenance to perform at the same
previous levels, until it breaks down completely and grinds to an
inevitable halt.

Take a practical example from your daily life. Let's say it is Friday
and you feel exhausted and say to yourself: 'Thank heavens I can now
rest for a couple of days.' During the weekend, you try to relax and
rest and do all the things that are normally fun, but suddenly they are
not. When Monday morning arrives you still feel like you did on the
Friday before the weekend – empty, unfulfilled and exhausted. If this
sounds familiar, you are heading for burnout. Burnout can strike

anyone, but it is often work-related. Although burnout can occur in any work situation, certain occupations seem to be particularly associated with it. For example, those who work with people on a daily basis, such as physicians, nurses, teachers and law enforcement officers, seem to be very vulnerable. Remember, just as the engine of your car will eventually seize up if it is not looked after and is driven beyond its capabilities, so you will end up in a stress-related emotional spiral (if you drive yourself relentlessly) which becomes such a vicious cycle that it eventually leads to total mental and physical exhaustion – commonly referred to as burnout.

TABLE 5.3

STAGES OF BURNOUT		
✓ OPTIMAL PERFORMANCE, COPING WITH STRESS		
✓ PAST OPTIMAL PERFORMANCE, STRESS TOO HIGH AND PROLONGED		
✓ DIMINISHED PRODUCTIVITY, EFFICIENCY, CREATIVITY, HEALTH, COMMUNICATION SKILLS, INTERPERSONAL SKILLS, AND SEXUAL ABILITY		
✓ PUSHING YOURSELF HARDER, POSSIBLY TAKING SUBSTANCES TO ACHIEVE THE SAME EARLIER OPTIMAL FUNCTIONING, RATHER THAN DEALING WITH STRESS. PSYCHOLOGICAL AND PHYSICAL WELL-BEING UNDERMINED BY THIS VICIOUS CYCLE		
☞ PHYSICAL AND PSYCHOLOGICAL EXHAUSTION, BURNOUT		

DEFENCE MECHANISMS AND STRESS REACTIONS

Various ways of coping with stress are discussed in Chapters 1 and 9. Coping can also be seen as task-oriented or defence-oriented reactions. Task-oriented reactions (much like problem-focused coping) involve making the necessary changes and adaptive behaviours to cope with stress. Defence-oriented reactions (much like emotion-focused coping) are directed primarily at protecting yourself from being psychologically damaged by stress. For example, typical basic defence-oriented reactions consist of emotional responses (crying, mourning, etc.) and the use of defence mechanisms (denial, repression, etc.). Although such reactions can be normal responses to stress, they can contribute to more stress if they become inappropriate or excessive.

Defence mechanisms (unconscious processes used to provide relief from emotional conflict and stress) are used by all of us during normal coping. In a way, they give us 'time-out' to help us deal with issues at hand and to make the necessary adjustments. But they can become problematic if used too often so that we never actually face the original problems. Psychological decompensation (a lowering of normal integrated functioning, deterioration of existing defences and psychological breakdown) can occur when your ego defence mechanisms become maladaptive or unhealthy and become the predominate means of coping with stress. The concept of ego-defence mechanisms was originally developed by Freud, but others have modified it since. They function a bit like psychological masks to hide true feelings.

COMMON DEFENCE MECHANISMS

Some of the more common defence mechanisms include:

* denial
* displacement (redirecting your feelings or thoughts towards another)
* intellectualisation (using intellectual activity to master your feelings)
* isolation
* projection (projecting your own undesirable thoughts or characteristics onto another)
* rationalisation (trying to offer rational explanations to justify your attitudes, beliefs or behaviour that might otherwise be unacceptable)
* regression (reverting to earlier modes of coping or thinking)
* repression (preventing your thoughts from getting into conscious awareness)
* sublimation (redirecting your feelings into some other worthwhile activity)
* suppression (postponement of threatening feelings from entering your conscious awareness)
* acting out (giving in to impulses to avoid the tension caused by postponing expression of the impulses)
* undoing (atoning for your previous behaviour in attempts to counteract the distress of immoral acts or desires)

GENERAL SIGNS AND SYMPTOMS OF UNHEALTHY STRESS

If you have a stress-related psychological disorder that you cannot cope with, you should seek appropriate professional help. However, I would like to recommend two simple techniques for you to assess and analyse your own general stress levels, because it is important to get a clear picture of the problems you have with stress which will assist you in finding solutions to cope. They are not intended for you to diagnose a psychological disorder, but to help you with negative stress. The first is using a checklist and the second involves keeping a stress record. Let's look at the first technique – a composite checklist of the general signs and symptoms of unhealthy stress, compiled from my own research, the literature and from patient complaints.

A checklist for analysing your stress

This checklist (Table 5.4) illustrates a variety of the signs and symptoms of stress, in order for you to identify and deal with them before you become a victim of a specific physical or psychological disorder related to your stress. According to this checklist, stress can be analysed by using the three systems approach based on the biopsychosocial and systems approach discussed earlier. The three systems involve an analysis of your physical reactions, psychological reactions and behavioural reactions which are also related to your social interactions because that is where you often express your behaviour. You are usually aware of your physical and psychological reactions, but your behavioural reactions are frequently observed by others who might comment on how your behaviour seems to have changed. It is necessary to be fairly specific about how stress affects you in each of these areas, and not to be vague about understanding your personal reactions to stress and what you can do about it, because each person reacts to stress in their own unique way. This will also help you get a clearer picture of why you experience the unpleasant symptoms that you have felt as a result of a stress response that you weren't even aware of. It is important to remember that some of these symptoms can arise from other causes (including medical and nutritional ones) which should also be considered.

TABLE 5.4

CHECKLIST OF THE GENERAL SYMPTOMS OF UNHEALTHY STRESS

Make a ✓ if you experience the symptoms *often* (at least once a week or more), and a ✗ if you experience it *sometimes* (less than weekly, but at least monthly). Do you experience:

PHYSICAL REACTIONS		
– UNUSUAL TIREDNESS	– HIGH BLOOD PRESSURE	– UNEXPLAINED NAUSEA
– APATHY/LACK OF ENTHUSIASM	– SEXUAL PROBLEMS	– FREQUENT INDIGESTION
– BREATHLESSNESS FOR NO REASON	– UNEXPLAINED HEADACHES/PAIN	– ERRATIC BOWEL FUNCTION
– FEELINGS THAT YOUR APPEARANCE HAS ALTERED FOR THE WORSE	– FEELING FAINT OR UNUSUALLY WEAK FOR NO REASON	– EXCESSIVE PERSPIRATION FOR NO REASON
– DIFFICULTY IN RELAXING	– MUSCLE TENSION	– DIZZY SPELLS FOR NO REASON
– DISTURBING DREAMS/ NIGHTMARES	– FEELING PHYSICALLY UNWELL	– FEELING TIGHT-CHESTED FOR NO REASON

PSYCHOLOGICAL REACTIONS		
– FEELINGS OF HELPLESSNESS	– FEELINGS OF DISLIKING YOURSELF	– FEELINGS THAT YOU ARE A FAILURE
– FEELINGS OF DEPRESSION	– BEING AFRAID OF DISEASE	– FEELING YOU CAN'T COPE
– FEELINGS THAT NO ONE UNDERSTANDS YOU	– AN INCREASE IN COMPLAINTS ABOUT WHAT HAPPENS TO YOU	– FEELINGS THAT OTHER PEOPLE DISLIKE YOU
– FEELINGS OF GENERAL ANXIOUSNESS	– LOW SELF-ESTEEM/LOW OPINION OF YOURSELF	– FEELINGS OF CONFUSION
– PHOBIAS (IRRATIONAL FEARS)	– FEELINGS OF BEING GOSSIPED ABOUT	– FEELINGS OF CONCERN MAINLY FOR YOURSELF
– AWKWARD FEELINGS WHEN CLOSE TO OTHERS	– BEING OVER SELF-CRITICAL	– FEELINGS OF FREQUENT CRITICISM
– FEELINGS THAT YOU HAVE FAILED IN YOUR ROLE AS A PARENT, SPOUSE, CHILD, EMPLOYEE, EMPLOYER	– FEELINGS THAT NO ONE WANTS TO WORK WITH YOU	– FEELINGS THAT YOU HAVE BEEN NEGLECTED OR LET DOWN
– PANICKY FEELINGS	– FEELING TENSE AND KEYED-UP	– FEELINGS OF LONELINESS AND NO ONE TO TALK TO
– BEING UPSET BY DISEASE IN OTHERS	– PERSISTENT GUILT	– A LACK OF SELF-CONFIDENCE

BEHAVIOURAL REACTIONS		
– MEMORY LOSS/ FORGETFULNESS	– DIFFICULTY IN MAKING UP YOUR MIND	– DISINTEREST IN OTHER PEOPLE
– POOR LONG-TERM PLANNING	– DIFFICULTY IN SHOWING/ EXPRESSING YOUR TRUE FEELINGS	– SUPPRESSED OR UNEXPRESSED ANGER
– POOR CONCENTRATION	– WORRYING	– FEARFULNESS
– INCONSISTENCY	– SOCIAL WITHDRAWAL	– POOR DECISION MAKING
– INABILITY TO MEET DEADLINES	– MAKING UNNECESSARY MISTAKES	– UNCO-OPERATIVE RELATIONSHIPS
– POOR TIME MANAGEMENT	– THE NEED TO REGULARLY WORK LATE	– FEELING DISGRUNTLED/ MOODY/ IRRITABLE
– PROCRASTINATION	– POOR WORK QUALITY	– EMOTIONAL OUTBURSTS
– THE NEED TO CONSTANTLY TAKE WORK HOME	– DIFFICULTY IN COMPLETING ONE TASK BEFORE RUSHING ON TO THE NEXT	– GREATER USE OF ALCOHOL, CAFFEINE, NICOTINE, MEDICINES TO COPE
– POOR PROBLEM-SOLVING SKILLS	– THE NEED TO CANCEL LEAVE	– FIDGETING/ RESTLESSNESS
– ACCIDENT-PRONENESS	– NAIL BITING	– UNPREDICTABILITY
– LOW INTEREST IN WORK	– AN EXCESSIVE APPETITE	– A LOSS OF APPETITE
– A DROP IN PERSONAL STANDARDS	– ENGAGING IN FREQUENT CRITICISM OF OTHERS	– THE NEED TO CRY FOR NO REASON
– INCREASED AGGRESSIVENESS	– FRANTIC BURSTS OF ENERGY	– TICS/NERVOUS HABITS
– LACK OF INTEREST IN LIFE	– LITTLE SENSE OF HUMOUR	– SLEEP DISTURBANCES

Scoring this checklist is simple. For every ✓ give yourself one point, and for every ✗ half a point. If your score is three or more for any one of the categories, then you are beginning to adapt to elements of stress in that particular category and should take the appropriate action. The higher your score, the more stressed you might be. Some of these symptoms could be the result of another cause (like disease, nutrition, etc) which you should take into account in your stress assessment. However, you will find that the symptoms in the checklist are mostly associated with stress. Look again at the stress curve to see where you fit (Figure 3.2).

A stress-monitoring record for analysing your stress

The second technique to analyse your reactions to stress involves self-monitoring by keeping a stress record. Self-monitoring is an excellent way of learning to cope with stress and means keeping a stress record by writing things down when they occur or as soon as possible afterwards, so that you can learn to assess your own individual stress reactions and how to help yourself cope with them. The information you gain from doing this exercise will help you to learn more about your own unique reactions to stress. Your stress record should follow the same three-systems analysis used in the checklist described previously – that is, you divide it into physical, psychological and behavioural reactions. You also need to look at the causes of the stress and your reactions in terms of antecedents and consequences.

A simple memory aid (ASC) derived from this concept can help with this:

A → ANTECEDENTS (What causes the stress)

S → STRESS REACTIONS (Your physical, psychological and behavioural reactions)

C → CONSEQUENCES (Anything that happens as a result of or after your stress reaction)

Now apply this to each of the three reactions you experience. So, by way of an example your stress record could look like the one illustrated in Table 5.5.

It is important to remember when you analyse your stress response like this, not to treat the antecedents, reactions and consequences as isolated events in your life. They are linked together and occur as being part of a chain of events that can also involve others. You have to consider the role of other people in your analysis. Also, make the analysis as simple as possible and if you do get confused, try and make it even simpler.

CONCLUSION

The reasons why people develop psychological disorders are complex. Many are caused by stress, but it would be too simple to attribute all their causes to stress, although stress can affect most psychological disorders. This is not surprising since stress affects the equilibrium of hormones and the neurochemicals in the brain which influence your psychological functioning and your behaviour. As with stress-related medical problems, in some cases stress makes some people more susceptible to certain psychological problems, and in others it makes existing ones worse.

TABLE 5.5

STRESS-MONITORING RECORD		
ANTECEDENTS	**STRESS REACTIONS**	**CONSEQUENCES**
Example 1 I was preparing to take a driving test.	1. PHYSICAL Muscle tension/ difficulty in relaxing	Headache
	2. PSYCHOLOGICAL Anxious/panicky feelings	Can't study
	3. BEHAVIOURAL Fearfulness/worrying/ fidgetiness	Cancelled the test!
Example 2 I have a problem in a relationship.	1. PHYSICAL Apathy/can't relax	High blood pressure/ physical tension
	2. PSYCHOLOGICAL Feeling like I can't cope/I'm not understood	Social withdrawal
	3. BEHAVIOURAL Aggresiveness/ unco-operative	Relationship worse

SUMMARY OF THE MAIN PRINCIPLES

- The causes of psychological disorders are complex and not all can be attributed to stress. Some are more specifically associated with stress than others.
- Stress does, however, affect most psychological disorders and can cause many general psychological problems.
- Specific psychological problems or disorders associated with stress can include: anxiety disorders, depressive disorders, suicidal behaviour, adjustment disorders, dissociative disorders, sleep disorders, sexual disorders, pain, somatoform disorders, factitious disorders, substance-related disorders, violence and burnout.
- Two basic techniques are recommended to assess and analyse your own general stress levels.
- The first one is a checklist of the general signs and symptoms of unhealthy stress which you can use to see which ones you suffer from.
- The second one is keeping your own stress-monitoring record.

CHAPTER 6

Identify your sources of stress

COMMON CAUSES OF STRESS

THE causes of stress cover a wide variety of conditions and, as we have seen, virtually any change or demand that you can't cope with (positive or negative) can induce stress. This can range from events as diverse as environmental exposure to extreme heat or cold, toxic compounds, radiation, pollution and other environmental irritants to pain, illness, injury, accidents, excitement, work issues, marriage, divorce, children or even surprises. Some authorities group stressors into three basic categories for the sake of convenience: frustrations, conflicts and pressures. All three involve a perception that they are stressful that can translate into negative thinking, emotional strain and stress. Frustrations occur when your strivings are thwarted and lead to feelings of failure or incompetence. Conflicts arise when your needs or motives are incompatible. Satisfying one desire means forfeiting the other. That is, you have choices to make and you experience conflict while trying to make what you perceive to be the right choice. Common conflicts are discussed in Chapter 12. Pressures stem from frustrations and conflicts, but also from the demand to achieve goals or to behave in certain ways. Pressures from within you or from your outside world force you to work harder to reach these ideals. As we saw earlier, various factors can influence the severity of stress and the degree of disruption it entails. For example, the nature of the stress, your perception of it, your thoughts about it, your stress tolerance, your age, your coping resources, your external resources and your psychosocial support systems could all play a role.

You might ask yourself: 'But are the pressures of daily life today really more stressful than in the past?' If you look back in the rearview mirror of that car that we are using as an example, do you see a less stressful road behind you compared to the road ahead? Isn't it a question of perception? We have discussed how some modern stress appears to be enjoyable to some, but not to others. On the other hand, we live in times of rapid change fired by a technological and computer-orientated society with all its excitement but daily frustrations. Change and the inability to cope with it has a lot to do with the problem of stress in modern society. As we move into a more stress-inducing, overcrowded, polluted, over-stimulated and technological future, change is likely to be even more rapid. Travelling, congested traffic, bad or inconsiderate drivers, pedestrians and overcrowded commuting contribute more stress to our daily lives today than ever before. Problems with political disruption and crises, increased urbanisation and mobility, unemployment and poverty, have all been identified as sources of stress. Depletion of natural resources, the ever-increasing domination of life by science, and the need to develop an inter-planetary point of view (when so many parts of the world are still starving or at war, etc.) commonly contribute to stress, as do negative social forces. It has become increasingly common these days in civil court cases to consider compensation for psychological damages as a result of stress. This is a difficult area that leaves room for considerable interpretation of the significance of the psychological stress and the causal link between it and the symptoms the person is presenting. It is also difficult to quantify the costs of such stress in monetary terms. If not handled circumspectly, though, it can be the precursor for even more stress. I cannot discuss all potential stressors here in depth, but let's look at a few common ones more closely.

Noise pollution

Incessant and overwhelming noise can be unhealthy and cause undue stress. Research has shown that children raised in excessively noisy environments often tend to have trouble discriminating between irrelevant noise and relevant (meaningful) noise. This can cause stress for children, their parents and their teachers. In adults, noise pollution can contribute to a host of problems, including cardiovascular problems, ulcers, irritability, fatigue and aggressiveness because of over-stimulation and altered levels of stress hormones. Research has even shown a reduction in testosterone levels in certain factory workers who are exposed to perpetual loud noise. Continuous noise can also have a negative, cumulative effect on hearing and result in noise-induced hearing loss in some people. Noise also causes irritation by decreasing the ability to concentrate. The most stressful noise, however, tends to be that which people cannot control. This was illustrated in my recent research on stress and the 'sick building syndrome', which clearly showed the damaging effects of noise and air pollution on people who regularly visit certain places of entertainment, such as clubs or music venues, where the noise from loud music can be incessant and overwhelming. An environmental monitoring system used in this research showed that comfort criteria for both noise and air pollution were often exceeded, which caused excessive stress in the people who worked there.

Anger

One of the many causes of stress in relationships relates to poor control of anger. People who lack anger management skills can over-react to such stressors, and their perceptions of the circumstances can make them reach 'boiling point'. The result can be the experience of stress levels which make them feel that they are literally beside themselves. In such situations one should aim for a level of anger display that is comfortable for all parties involved. It is not healthy to always suppress anger unduly, but anger inappropriately displayed can make the stress worse, and even lead to aggressive behaviour that might end up in physical harm and more stress. Effective communication and conflict resolution skills can assist to prevent this. This will help with the frequent feeling that you are being 'attacked', or that you are always 'on defence'. Such feelings that your personal domain is being unjustifiably attacked, can lead you to perceive that your territory is being invaded and that your psychological or physical space is being crowded. This in turn can create the perception that something is being taken away without your consent, and so the vicious cycle of anger and aggressive outbursts continue – causing more stress.

Techno-stress

Apart from the cyber stress and Internet addiction discussed further on, in our modern world with its high technology environment, stress is a common response to information overload. It was initially thought that technology would make life easier. Although this might be so, in some cases the opposite is true. Work loads have become heavier, deadlines tighter and interpersonal and human contact less. The result is more stress. The effect of the knowledge explosion and increased computerisation has literally reorganised our social and economic systems. In the process, confusion about ever-new and more complicated technology and the rapid changes that accompany it can contribute to stress. So can working with computerised equipment. Not only does one have to stay abreast of developments, but as soon as a computer or cell-phone is updated, a new, more modern one appears on the market. Another example is the impact of stress on using the equipment. Two examples are computer terminal workers who develop complaints of eye strain, backache, headache, tension, and even decreased mental alertness, and motor car accidents that are increasingly being reported as a result of drivers using their cell-phones without car kits while simultaneously driving their cars in busy traffic.

CYBER STRESS AND INTERNET ADDICTION

Recent research has highlighted the fact that techno-stress can contribute to increasing feelings of isolation. For example, the very technology that is supposed to keep people in close contact with work colleagues, family and friends is replacing vital everyday human interaction. Some studies have shown that heavy use of the Internet can result in an increasing sense of guilt and loneliness because it diminishes social support or interpersonal interaction. You cannot get a hug or a true sense of belonging from a computer. Research has clearly demonstrated the positive effects of a daily hug, and the fact that a kiss and a cuddle under the right circumstances can be a real elixir of life. Although there are clear benefits in 'techno-communication', the progressive imbalance created between human and electronic communication can create stress-related problems. Take two simple examples: what are the psychological implications routed in the difference between talking face-to-face to someone as opposed to constantly using a piece of technology such as telephones or e-mail?; and how does technology such as excessive use of the Internet interfere with life's normal activities?

Internet addiction has been described in medical journals as a condition that can wreak havoc in relationships and cause physical problems in obsessive users. Internet addiction covers a wide range of behaviours, such as: cyber sexual and cyber pornography addiction; cyber-relationship problems where cyber affairs and on-line friendships replace real-life relationships; Internet compulsion characteristic of obsessive on-line trading and gambling; compulsive web surfing or data base searches resulting in information overload; and computer addiction associated with obsessive computer use or playing of computer games. Physical symptoms of Internet addiction include: sleep deprivation; eye-strain; backache; and carpal tunnel syndrome (where the nerve in the wrist is compressed resulting in pain and numbness in the fingers or weakness of the thumb). Some people use the Internet to escape from psychological problems and stress that are not adequately dealt with, resulting in more stress.

Population explosion

Although the population explosion can contribute to stress, crowds themselves are not necessarily stressful. But, as in the case of noise, crowds tend to be stressful when they affect our sense of control and freedom – that is, not when we are crowded but when we feel crowded. Urbanisation is also a major problem. Health organisations have warned that without adequate planning the growth of mega-cities will constitute one of the biggest threats to public health in the 21st century. Predictions are that by the year 2025 about 75 per cent of the world's population will be urbanised, especially in developing countries where the percentage could be much higher. Even Africa, which has overwhelmingly rural populations, will become a predominantly urbanised society. As the baby boomers age, so the residents of nursing homes increase. Projected figures for some industrialised countries show that the number of nursing home residents over 65 years is likely to increase by up to 66 per cent between the years 1990 to 2020. These trends in population shifts could create direct health threats, but also enormous stress because of overcrowding, lack of housing and problems in providing basic infrastructure. There seems little doubt that the population increase and resultant big socio-economic squeeze will add further stress.

Violence
Lately violence has been much in the news, and many people have become familiar with the stress it causes. Violence is a human phenomenon that is deeply enmeshed in interpersonal interaction. It tends to be socially learnt behaviour and breeds itself. That is, it can spread and perpetuate itself. Frequently, interpersonal violence occurs between people who know each other as opposed to inter-group violence that often involves strangers. Violence in society occurs at different levels and in many various forms. Some types include political violence, legal violence as in corporal or capital punishment, violent crimes, violence in sport, domestic violence that involves children and family members, violence in schools, violence in places of detention, violence associated with alcohol and substance abuse, trauma, brain injury, certain diseases, psychological disorders, sexual violence, television violence, etc. Exposure to violence can also result in psychological disorders such as those discussed in Chapter 5. For example, there is evidence that exposure to human violence could have a more severe post-traumatic stress impact on the victim than exposure to a natural trauma such as earthquakes and floods.

Not only is violence in the community implicated in stress, but so too is violence in the workplace, which seems to have increased significantly. If you want to deal with work-related violence, it is important as a first step to acknowledge its existence. The days seem to be gone when work-related violence was only associated with certain occupational hazards such as sometimes noted in the work of psychiatric nurses, prison wardens, police officers and soldiers. Recent research has shown that violence can erupt in any workplace setting and that the stress that leads to such violence can be caused by both work violence as well as domestic violence that can spill over into the workplace. Even in general hospitals violence has become a problem. It is prudent to bear in mind that people who threaten violence or who become violent are often unable to cope with unbearable stress.

Nutrition

Nutrition is a critical factor in stress. What and when you eat affects your general health, and good health is important in stress management. Elevated cholesterol levels have recently been associated with stress, and the health protective roles of antioxidant vitamins, minerals and beta-carotene in disease prevention has been highlighted by major international studies. They play a role in the prevention of diverse disease processes including cancer and heart disease. In addition, over- or under-eating, or inappropriate or inadequate consumption of food, are important considerations. We now know that inadequate dietary habits can contribute to stress, especially when there is vitamin and mineral depletion in the diet. At the same time stress can contribute to the depletion of essential nutrients in the body. When you are stressed the food you consume may not provide enough essential nutrients to cope. This in turn produces more stress. A common example of how diet can influence stress is hypoglycaemia (a deficiency of glucose in the blood) which is characterised by anxiety, headache, dizziness, sweating, breathlessness, blurred vision, trembling, increased heart activity and reduced concentration – all of which can lower stress tolerance levels.

Another, often overlooked aspect, is that the consumption of certain foods can contribute to the stress of daily hassles, because they contain substances like preservatives and stimulants that actually mimic the stress response. By ignoring this you can contribute to the cumulative effect of an unhealthy diet and other stress in your life.

Perhaps one of the more important aspects of stress and diet relates to brain function and the need for brain food to cope with stress. Your perception of stress and thoughts about it are functions of your brain. Your brain needs energy to keep it operating smoothly and efficiently. For the most part, the fuel for this energy comes from your diet. Just as your car needs the right kind and amount of fuel to continue to perform when you drive it, so you need the right kind and amount of food (fuel) to perform optimally. The brain can store very little in the way of nutrients it requires and has constant energy demands. This voracious appetite continues unabated even when you sleep, and it is important to eat correctly for optimal brain maintenance. Although the brain comprises only two per cent of body weight in the average adult, it uses some 20 per cent of the total energy consumption of the body and, apart from other nutrients, almost all vitamins and minerals are needed by the brain for its proper functioning.

Some nutrients are more essential than others, but generally a well-balanced diet is a first step towards overall physical and mental health. During stress, increased supplies of certain nutrients are needed. You often have less of an appetite at such times because your body knows that more energy is urgently needed for the 'fight-or-flight' response than, let's say, for searching for and eating food. Even if you do eat more when you are stressed, you may not be able to get the full benefit of this extra food, since the blood supply in your body during the stress-induced arousal state has been re-directed to your body's muscles to maximise strength and reaction time. The stomach and intestines may even react negatively to solid food causing nausea and vomiting. Conversely, not eating sufficient food can also be a problem because most people under stress secrete extra acid in the stomach, which can contribute to the development of ulcers in certain people if they do not eat adequately.

When some people are stressed they eat too much. This is partly because eating is a familiar activity that takes their mind off the stress, and possibly also because the food they consume can contribute to the release of soothing substances in the brain such as certain neurotransmitters (chemicals in the nervous system that help with the transmission of impulses and act like messengers). Sometimes stress can cause an increased production of morphine-like substances in the brain (called endorphines) which can promote eating and the reduction of certain activity. On the other hand, some people develop eating disorders. Examples of well-described and frequently stress-related eating disorders are: obesity; anorexia nervosa (a disturbance of body image and the pursuit of thinness – sometimes to the point of starvation); and bulimia nervosa (binge-eating or eating of large amounts of food accompanied by feelings of being out of control, guilt, depression, or self-disgust, and behaviours such as self-induced vomiting, abuse of laxatives, or diuretics, fasting and/or excessive exercise).

As you now know, when you experience high stress levels, normal dietary sources of vitamins and minerals may not always be adequate, and higher intake of these and other indispensable nutrients are essential as their depletion further lowers your ability to cope with stress and predisposes you to further health problems. Vitamins and mineral deficiencies are in themselves linked to various medical disorders, and replenishment of depleted nutrients is not only especially important after a period of great stress, but also following recovery from disease. Remember, when your body and brain are properly nourished and you feel healthy and your thinking is clear, you can rise to the challenges of stress and work out better solutions to its causes and management.

HEALTHY EATING

You should aim for a variety of natural foods with as few additives as possible, adequate amounts of dietary fibre, reduced cholesterol intake and reduced sugar and salt intake. You should eat plenty of fresh fruit and vegetables, and reduce foods that can trigger the stress response (such as caffeine-containing foods or foods with other stimulants), alcohol and other harmful substances. You will deal better with stress if you cultivate a diet that comprises adequate amounts of essential nutrients including minerals and vitamins, and a balanced calorie intake in relation to energy output, as well as an overall healthy eating style which incorporates eating slowly and regularly.

Work environment

The work environment can feature prominently in stress at all levels of all job descriptions – not just at senior levels of management. There has been an enormous amount of research into occupational and organisational stress in the last few years, since for most economically active people, stress can be work-related. Such stress generally refers to the response of a person to stress in the work environment, whatever the cause. This is often referred to as work pressure, and there are many so called 'pressure points' related to employment and/or unemployment. Low morale and absenteeism are clear indicators of stress in the workplace, and management styles and management systems, as well as organisational factors, can affect the incidence and prevalence rates of such work stress. Environmental factors at work can add to the problem, and certain types of employment can actually determine the types of diseases the person contracts. These are referred to as occupational diseases.

According to research, some of the more common sources of stress that you can experience at work are associated with your occupation itself, your role in the organisation, your career development, your relationships at work, the organisational structure and the psychological climate. These are 'part and parcel' of the work situation itself or the work environment, and often have to do with poor physical working conditions, work overload, work pressures and taking responsibility for other people's lives.

Occupational stress can also be associated with an increase in accidents at work and, therefore, affect both work safety and productivity. Sometimes stress can arise from your role within the organisation, which has to do with issues such as not knowing quite what your work role is (role ambiguity) and consequently conflict arises, an overlapping of boundaries occurs and your own image of your occupational profile suffers in the process. Inadequate or inappropriate job descriptions are often at the very basis of stress and frustrations. In such situations people find that they are expected to perform tasks that they have little or no training for, that were never in their employment descriptions or even worse, that they are not getting adequately paid for.

Stress caused by problems surrounding career development frequently has to do with a lack of promotion, overpromotion, thwarted ambitions or a lack of work security. In pressing socio-economic times, work security becomes a major problem for many workers and their families, who they have to support. This latter point is made worse by scarcity of employment opportunities and difficulty in finding suitable employment. In such circumstances many people who are well-educated and skilled are leaving school, college and university but can't find work. The perception that they are entering a phase of unemployment doldrums can be extremely stressful. High levels of unemployment in a society can also lead to social unrest and strike action in support of colleagues who have lost their jobs. This occurs especially if the perception exists that they were unfairly dismissed, or that a depletion of the workforce is harmful to the economic survival of the able bodied in the community. The latter is sometimes linked to techno-stress because of advanced automation and computerisation which is revolutionising the ratio of labour to capital in many production processes, and so contributes in some cases to an employment downturn which may further worsen social tensions and stress. Rapid technological change and progress, volatile financial markets, highly competitive trade, company mergers, take-overs and economic recession are all potential stress-inducing factors that are debated in the media daily.

Many executives and middle managers function under constant pressure. Such pressure can motivate them to perform well, but when it becomes relentless and unrealistic it switches from being a motivator to a stressor, thereby making the work environment a stressful situation. They feel that they are being controlled, rather than being in control. The results are the common reactions described in this book as negative stress.

A positive psychological climate in the workplace is vital if stress is to be kept to a minimum. Difficulties in work relationships can be very stressful, such as a poor relationship with the boss, or with your subordinates or colleagues, or if there are work-related difficulties in delegating responsibilities. Research has shown, for example, that if the psychological climate in a medical unit or a hospital ward is healthy, patients respond better to the medical treatment than they would if the psychological climate was unhealthy. The same principle applies to the work situation. The stress levels of a company are easily reflected in the stress levels of its employees – its most valuable resource. Just as individuals can find themselves in the positive or negative phase of the stress curve with its positive or negative consequences, so can a company. The way a company manages its stress directly influences its quality of output. A company should aim for holistic company health to achieve optimal performance. Each part or sub-system of the company forms a part of the whole. Although independent, they are all interdependent and the one affects the other. In as much as you cannot split mind and body in people, so you cannot split the 'mind and body' of a company. To be effective it has to function holistically. Stress management should address sources of stress at all levels of the system to achieve the best possible results. According to researchers, three categories of people who are particularly vulnerable to work stress are those who have low levels of control and decision-making at work, which results in feelings of boredom and helplessness, those who have low levels of control but high levels of responsibilities, and those who have powerful needs to be in control.

To test whether you are experiencing work stress ask yourself the questions in Table 6.1. If your answer is yes to even one, I suggest that you try to address the problem immediately to avoid further stress.

Now, if you couple your unresolved personal problems or home problems with the types of stress-inducing work problems discussed here, it could lead not only to more stress resulting in poor psychological and physical well-being or even disease, but also, within the company, to poor productivity, high labour turnover and sometimes even industrial action such as strikes. Why? Because stress at home can affect stress at work, and vice versa. What can you do in this situation? It is important to accept that stress management is the responsibility of both the organisation and the individual working for it, and that the welfare of the worker extends to the welfare of the worker's family and social life. You can't separate these issues in good stress management. Ask yourself: 'What help would you offer should you be confronted with such negative stress situations?' You need to do this against the backdrop of understanding what constitutes negative stress, how to identify it, what stress management involves, and understanding that stress management is part of both good business practice and lifestyle management. This implies a concern for the welfare of the company, its management and its employees. A first step, though, is for you to be able to identify the stressors in your own life and deal with them.

TABLE 6.1

ARE YOU EXPERIENCING WORK STRESS?
✓ Are you simply a number that could easily be replaced and do you feel that you have no participation in, for example, company policy or the decision-making process?
✓ Are your company objectives and goals unclear?
✓ Are there too many restrictions placed on your budget or on your behaviour for you to function effectively at a high productivity level?
✓ Are you stressed by office politics and tense interpersonal relationships at work?
✓ Do you feel there is no team spirit?
✓ Is it more dangerous for you to leave your office to go and have a glass of water, than it would be to cross a busy street in the city because you are afraid that your character might be assassinated in the process?
✓ Do you feel that you don't work in an environment of mutual and reciprocal trust and support?
✓ Do you feel a lack of effective consultation?
✓ Is it your perception that you have lost control in your work situation, or that you are losing control and that you are heading for burnout?

Personality types

Apart from actual working conditions, high stress levels can be maintained by certain personality characteristics. For example, some people are always in a state of stress and can always find something to worry about – the so-called 'stress-prone personalities'. Another example, the Type A personality, which is characterised by a sense of work-related time urgency or 'hurry-sickness', is perhaps the most widely quoted in this respect. Research has linked the Type A personality to coronary-prone behaviour, much of which centres around an intense need to maintain control at all costs. In this process the cardiovascular system can become a prime target for the stress response. The Type A personality refers to a constant struggle to achieve, an impatience at anyone or anything that gets in the way, irritability and an intense effort to control the environment. Although these traits can be manifested elsewhere in the Type A person's life, they are often clearly demonstrated in the workplace. This Type A behaviour pattern is associated with increased reactivity to stress and tends to represent an ongoing process of creating challenges to which the person must respond. Such a person engages in constant demands which can produce negative health results and become a potential risk factor for physical disorders such as heart disease. But it has other ramifications as well, and may even make the Type A person more prone to accidents and interpersonal conflict. Not all Type A characteristics are necessarily associated with health problems, but particularly hazardous traits have been shown to be an aggressiveness coupled with anger, resentment and hostility. The aggressive component appears to be a particularly toxic link with health problems.

As opposed to this, the Type B person is less intense and has a more slow-moving and easy-going manner, is slower to be aroused by anger and is generally more relaxed. Whereas Type A behaviour constitutes a continuous emotional disquiet associated with an abnormally intense, chronic struggle to achieve more in less time and exaggerated hostile actions to various activities of others, Type B lacks these components.

Psychology researchers have also written about the Type C behaviour pattern which comprises a coping style of excessive passivity, co-operativeness and emotional non-expression. The Type C coper finds it extremely difficult to express anger and presents to the world a facade of contentment. Such people are often self-sacrificing in the extreme and are more concerned about others' needs than their own. Unlike Type A and B personalities, this appears to be more a behaviour pattern and coping style than a personality type. The Type C's characteristic behaviour pattern and style of coping with stress have been shown to be a possible factor in certain diseases such as, for example, the progression of cancer.

Family stress

Many issues can cause family stress. Three good examples are family disputes, depriving a child (or family unit) of the mother or father's needed input, and mothers who hold down full-time jobs.

Constant family bickering can contribute to serious problems. If the resultant stress is not addressed and allowed to spiral out of control the consequences can be far reaching, even resulting in disruption of the family unit, violence or grave psychological consequences. For example, results from my research showed that one of the most significant stressors that could end up in suicidal behaviour was frequent interpersonal conflict involving a key person in the life of the suicidal patient. This was so for by far the most adolescents and adults studied who were suicidal. The adolescents predominantly reported frequent parent–child problems, and those over the age of 20 predominantly complained of frequent conflict in their love or marital relationships. Family-related social predicaments, unemployment, financial difficulties, and accommodation and legal problems were also important stressors in these suicidal patients.

Maternal or paternal deprivation can affect a young child's development. The negative effects of not having a close, supportive relationship with a father, mother or both are well known. Lack of parental affection (especially maternal care and affection) can trigger the release of high levels of stress hormones in babies and young children which can negatively affect their development and performance. For example, research has shown abnormally high levels of cortisone (a hormone released during high stress) in abandoned babies and children in overcrowded and understaffed orphanages. Sometimes the absence of such a relationship may even be profoundly experienced where the father is not physically absent from the family but psychologically absent (as in not being 'involved'), and as a result the parent–child relationship suffers severely. While earlier psychological research focused particularly on the negative effects of the absence of the mother in a child's life, later work has shown that the absence of a father can also have negative consequences. These issues contribute to stress in the child and its parents if not adequately dealt with.

The multiple roles of the 'working mother' are the focus of much psychological attention these days, because of the stress these women suffer. In certain communities the majority of mothers are economically active. Questions commonly beckoning answers are: 'Does being employed as well as being a mother enhance or threaten a woman's health, especially her psychological well-being?' 'What impact would such stress have on her children?' Some psychological research has suggested that because of limited time and energy, women with such competing demands can suffer from overload and role stress (stress caused by the need to play too many roles simultaneously). There is also significant potential for conflict: on the one hand multiple roles can contribute to stress, but on the other hand this can provide greater self-esteem, financial and social support. However, these latter gains are offset by increased stress and related pressures, which can be made worse by the additional time women are required to spend on the 'unpaid' hours they work at home. Strictly speaking, raising children and running a home when a woman is economically active constitutes, as it were, a form of 'unpaid overtime'. For example, researchers have shown that in some cases working women spend up to 90 hours a week in such 'unpaid' work as opposed to the typical 60 hours a week of their male counterparts. On top of that, some working mothers have to put in paid overtime at their places of employment. Their stress levels can then soar because the stressors in their lives are cumulative, in that home and work stressors combine to put them more at risk of stress-related problems.

WORKING ROLES

Research shows that some men resent it when their wives flourish in their careers, especially when such men are stressed about their own careers or are thinking about retirement. Many women find a new lease in their working lives and social circles at such times and when their children have left home. This can lead to a shift in the power balance of the relationship. This in turn, can affect the self-confidence of these men, which could lead to sexual and other problems because of resultant feelings of inadequacy. Work is often motivated by a combination of intrinsic (pleasure in doing the work, intellectual challenges or curiosity) and extrinsic (reward and praise) factors. An understanding of these factors can assist in decreasing stress that might arise in couple relationships because of changes in working roles.

Further, many professional women have to put their careers either 'on hold' or 'on half-time' for some years so that they have more time to devote to their families, thereby creating a further potential for frustration, conflict and stress. In fact, some highly talented women are deprived of developing a successful career because of family commitments, and can only find the time for it after their children are grown up. Many women also do not make career provisions for the effects of the 'empty-nest syndrome', which typically occurs after their children have left home and when they can experience a profound sense of loss, resulting in stress.

Lack of physical activity

A sedentary and physically inactive and unstimulating lifestyle can be stressful, because not only is the body designed for physical action, but a healthy body contributes to wellness and a better quality of life. In fact, the 'fight-or-flight' response was intended to produce physical activity to cope with stress. It follows that a natural way to take care of the 'fight-or-flight' response (to help neutralise the stress response) is through appropriate physical activity. Such activity (like exercise programmes or sport) is important not only as a 'treatment' for the stress response, but also prevents stress and produces a sense of well-being which helps the person to be more stress-resistant. There is plenty of new research showing that appropriate exercise can produce significant psychological benefits such as elevating a person's mood and relieving depression and anxiety. To achieve the necessary benefits, however, requires a regular exercise pattern, and not just a 'one off' effort. It is important, though, that such physical activity does not become a stressor in itself, which usually happens when it becomes highly competitive and the primary aims are to feed an undernourished 'ego' or to make as much money as possible from it, rather than to produce a sense of well-being and reduce stress. An over-inflated ego leads to excessive 'ego-involvement' in whatever the person does. This can cause more stress, while the aim is to avoid this and to seek a balance between physical and psychological (mental) activity and well-being.

Commuting stress

The modern day commuting experience can have far-ranging impacts on physical and psychological health, and the movement of people resulting in mass transportation has become an increasing focus of psychological research. For example, road rage (and recently air rage) and commuting stress have become the malaise of modern time, leading to significant further stress. Road users sometimes suffer real or imagined 'slights' and intimidation from other drivers, and because of a stress response over-react. The same happens at busy airports and on long international flights. The resultant disproportionate outrage and behavioural response has come to be known as the syndrome of road rage or air rage. Increased volumes of traffic, time pressures and the tendency of commuters to act out their stress and frustration on the roads and in air travel, as they compete for increasingly congested travel space and demanding time schedules, are major considerations in the syndrome. During long-distance transmeridian flights the problem can be aggravated by 'jet lag' and disturbances in the sleep–wake cycle (circadian rhythm) because of the need to adjust to new time zones. Such flights are usually non-smoking, with passengers who are addicted to nicotine going through withdrawal symptoms, thus further complicating stress control. Recent media reports have also focused on the hazards of alcohol abuse on long flights, resulting in air rage. Such issues, in turn, have resulted in an associated syndrome called commuting stress. The negative effects on physical and psychological health can be serious and a whole range of conditions have been traced to commuting stress, including the effects of exhaust fumes, pollution, back pain, noise, screaming drivers, high traffic volumes, long queues, overbookings and flight delays, and the consequences of accidents. Research has shown that false perceptions can be created when drivers feel safely cacooned from the outside world inside their vehicles, and that some drivers show characteristics of territorial behaviour. For example, if they are 'cut off' by another driver or if somebody sits too close on their tail, this could be perceived as an invasion of personal road space and a challenge to defend it. The result could be an aggressive response very much like the way animals behave in nature when strangers invade their territory. If it happens to you, how would you feel? If it happens on the way home, how would it affect your relationships with your loved ones welcoming you back? If it happens on your way to work, how would it affect your work or the rest of your day? Drivers are often over-anxious to point out the bad driving behaviour of others and do not take into account their own. They also frequently fail to realise that commuting is not simply a matter of getting from point A to point B, but that they should do so responsibly and safely. This involves taking into account their own perceptions, thoughts, feelings and commuting behaviour, as well as those of other road users. Likewise, pedestrians frequently place responsibility for their road safety on drivers, rather than accepting personal responsibility for it. So, bear in mind that the way you respond on the road and the way you manage road rage and your stress could be critical to your safety – and that of others. Stay calm and enjoy your commuting.

Daily hassles

Apart from life events and more enduring problems which could lead to prolonged or repeated stress, researchers have noted more recently that some of the most common sources of stress are rooted in the pressures of daily life – these include those little, but numerous, daily hassles such as time pressures, paying bills, family conflict and so on. The build-up of daily hassles and being constantly pounded by them can sometimes be more stressful than a single great stressful event. How you permit such hassles to affect your life depends on your perception of them and your coping skills.

CONCLUSION

Successful coping does not mean a life without any problems and a life without stress. You have to learn problem-solving techniques and stress management skills, rather than aiming for a stress-free existence. Stress will always exist, but try not to feel overwhelmed and helpless or overcome by feelings of anxiety, depression and pessimism. Probably one of the most powerful stressors is the perception that you have lost control of your life. It doesn't matter whether you have or not, or whether it is real or imagined, it is essentially your perception that you have lost control that makes you feel overwhelmed.

So far you have learnt some of the first basic steps in identifying and understanding stress. In the next part of this book we'll look at some practical methods to deal with it based on changing your perception of the stress in your life and other stress management skills. Just like you have to sometimes make a gear shift to control your car better, so you sometimes have to make a perceptual shift to control your stress better. Never forget – if you don't do this, the negative effects of stress can last for periods long after the actual stress is over.

SUMMARY OF THE MAIN PRINCIPLES

- It is important for you to identify the sources of stress in your life.
- The causes of stress cover a wide range.
- Stressors involve a perception that they are stressful that translates into stress.
- Life events and enduring problems can lead to prolonged stress.
- Daily hassles can sometimes be more stressful than a major single stressful event.
- What causes stress for you does not necessarily cause stress for others.
- Certain personality characteristics can maintain high stress levels.

Part Three

What can you do about it?

A key issue in the management of stress is to take control and put yourself back into the 'psychological driving seat'. You must be in psychological control, rather than feeling that you are being controlled. There are various techniques that you can apply to achieve this.

CHAPTER 7

Change your perception

ACHIEVING PSYCHOLOGICAL SELF-EMPOWERMENT

STRESS and change are inevitable. So, what can you do about it if you can't avoid it? You can learn to cope with it and make it work for you, not against you. Stress and change are not necessarily all bad and can, in fact, sometimes be desirable. How do you achieve this? Because stress can produce a sense of being overwhelmed and leave you with a feeling that you are not in control, you have to start by changing aspects of yourself to achieve self-empowerment. That is, you've got to take control and put yourself back in the 'psychological driving seat' of life or a situation that was rapidly speeding out of control. A crucial initial step in this process is to change your perception, so that you can better utilise the basic stress stoppers. The need to make the necessary perceptual shift is a critical first requirement in stress management, because you will have difficulty in empowering yourself psychologically to cope with stress unless you change your perception about stress and its effects on you. Any stress-producing perceptions should be changed and less damaging ones should be used to replace them. You can change your thinking, feelings and behaviour when you change perceptions.

The need to change your perceptions about various stress-related issues arises frequently in this book. This is so because stressful experiences alone do not cause stress. It is particularly your perception of the experiences that does. There are always different ways of looking at the same problem. Proverbially speaking 'every medal has its reverse' and 'there are two sides to every question'. This is also true for the stressors in your life. If you fail to see this because you rigidly stick only to your perception (or misperception) that causes the stress, you'll miss the stress management boat. So, changing your perception can help you to change positively, because what you see and the tool you use to see it with (perception) will then be more in harmony. By altering your perception, you effectively change the negative consequences of the stressor on you. The reason is that your perception of a stressor has a powerful influence on how you interpret and react to the stress it causes in your life. Thus, you can change the harmful effects that stress has on you by changing the way you 'see' the stress.

95

Making this necessary perceptual shift will modify your thinking patterns. Your thinking in turn determines your emotions and feelings, which in turn affect your behaviour and stress response. You have heard the saying 'get in touch with your feelings'. People say this because feelings affect behaviour. But to really get in touch with your feelings, you first have to get in touch with your perceptions and your thoughts. To assist you with this, let's start with a useful memory aid derived from the very word 'perception' – PERCEB:

PER → PERCEPTION
C   → COGNITIONS (THOUGHTS)
E   → EMOTIONS
B   → BEHAVIOUR

When you want to change your perception of the stressor to manage your stress more effectively, remember the memory aid PERCEB and what it stands for.

Perception

Perception is a psychological function that enables you to receive, process and interpret information about your environment. It is not the same as sensation. Sensation is the simple registration of sensory phenomena by your senses – that is, information is received by your brain directly from your senses. You then have to interpret this information so that it is meaningful to you. Not everybody interprets the same information in the same way, and you can also 'read' it differently at different times. Humans have six known senses that convey information to the brain. They are sight, hearing, smell, touch, taste and proprioception (the sense that provides information about the internal state of the body, such as the muscles, the skeleton and the movement of the body called kinetics). These senses evolved to help you survive, because you do not simply note events in your environment – you also give them meaning. That is, you do not only register what your senses tell you, you interpret it.

The brain's powers of interpretation are so strong that people can even adjust to abnormal images. This interpretation involves perception as a higher level process which makes sense of your sensations because what you see, hear, smell, touch or feel will depend not only on external or internal stimuli but also on how you decode this information based on your experiences, personality, needs, etc. In a way, your senses feed your brain the raw data and your forebrain organises the data into coherent patterns – coherent for you, that is. This synthesis of data by your brain also involves your beliefs, attitudes, thoughts, etc. when you are awake, and your dreams when you are asleep. Although perception involves the way you experience and interpret the world around you, sensations are your first steps to such conscious awareness. Perception is the process by which sensory impulses are 'read' by your brain to organise and interpret them. This includes the interpretation of stressors in your life. A certain amount of sensory and perceptual stimulation is necessary for normal functioning, but too much can be overwhelming and too little can lead to serious problems.

Attention is an important part of perception because it involves the process of selecting particular information that you interpret. A key process in selective attention is 'filtering' or 'blocking'. This can give you some control over what you want to see. You sometimes filter or block out certain aspects of sensory information. For example, if you are driving your car, you will ignore or discard certain disturbing interferences so that you can focus on the task in hand – safely driving the car. Other factors that play a role in this regard are your motives, needs and interests. If you are aiming for a certain destination or if you are in the market to buy a new car, these factors will influence your actions and choices on how to get to your destination or how to go about acquiring the new car. To make sense of your world you must be able to understand where things begin and end for you. This is where a problem can arise when it comes to stress, because the sense you make of your world can sometimes be based on wrong perceptions that cause you stress. Let's say you buy that new car because you have the perception that it will meet your needs. Once you've owned and driven it for a while, you become aware that your perception was completely wrong – you can't afford the repayments, it's too expensive to maintain, the service back-up is poor, or whatever else is wrong. These issues now cause you untold stress.

Although there are various different senses, I will focus on visual perception as an example of how perceptions can be misinterpreted because much research has been concentrated in this area. Modern cognitive psychology (the psychology of thinking processes) has its roots in the earlier Gestalt and behaviourist traditions and in cognitive science and information processing. The Gestalt psychologists were among the first to study visual perception and how we organise what we see into meaningful units and patterns. Their motto was: 'The whole is different from the sum of its parts.' The German word 'gestalt' means 'pattern' or 'configuration'. They identified a set of principles of perception which involve, amongst others, concepts about similarity, proximity, closure, continuity and figure-ground organisation.

- According to the principle of similarity, if all things are equal, we will automatically perceive the similar ones as belonging together.
- According to the principle of proximity, if things are close to each other, we see them as forming a group.
- According to the principle of closure, we tend to prefer seeing closed figures rather than fragmented or unconnected ones.
- According to the principle of continuity, we tend to smooth out irregularities in an object.

Good 'gestalt' affects our perception because of our preference for less fragmentation. These and other principles help us to understand how we create good 'gestalts' in the way we see things. We might have a different appreciation in our perception of certain types of art, but generally in life we tend to recognise well-rounded, good 'gestalt' figures more easily. All this results in a tendency for us to see things in terms of figure-ground organisation (or perception) – that is, we tend to perceive things in terms of figures, objects or events as standing out clearly against their backgrounds. Examples are a car travels on a road, pedestrians walk on a sidewalk, pictures hang on a wall or the words you are reading are on a page. These principles of perception are illustrated in Figures 7.1 to 7.5.

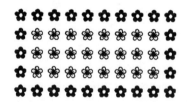 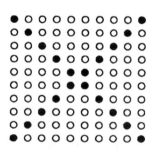

FIGURE 7.1 *The principle of similarity. Because of our tendency to group things together that are similar in size, shape, colour or form, we tend to see two groups of flowers in the illustration on the left, rather than one rectangular bed of flowers, and an X in the illustration on the right, rather than a single square of dots and circles – things that are alike in some way tend to be perceived as belonging together.*

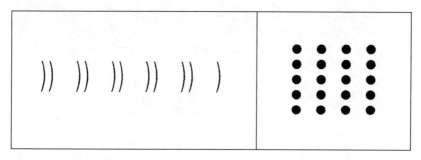

FIGURE 7.2 *The principle of proximity. Because of our tendency to group things together that are near each other, we tend to see five pairs of brackets and a single one, rather than 11 brackets, and the dots as four vertical strings, rather than 20 separate dots.*

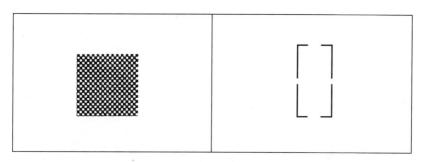

FIGURE 7.3 *The principle of closure. Because of our tendency to close gaps so that we see complete forms, we tend to see a single big square rather than separate tiny squares on the left, and a complete rather than broken rectangle on the right.*

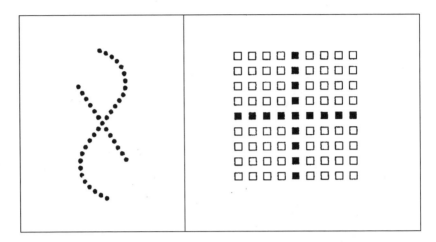

FIGURE 7.4   *The principle of continuity.* *Because we tend to see lines and patterns as continuing, we tend to smooth out irregularities in objects that we see. In these figures we tend to see two lines (one straight and one curved) instead of four lines (two curved and two straight) on the left, and on the right two lines crossing, rather than four lines coming together in the middle.*

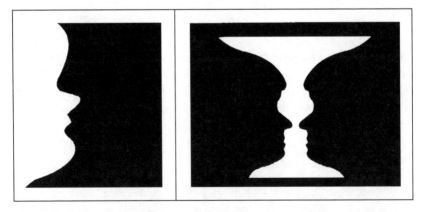

FIGURE 7.5   *Figure-ground perception.* *Each of these figures can be interpreted in two possible ways. The one on the left includes two different faces shaped by the same contour. The one on the right can be seen as two silhouettes or a vase.*

Much of the earlier work on perception centred around visual illusions (*ignis fatuus*) or misperceptions, examples of which are illustrated in Figures 7.6 to 7.12. Illusions are useful to illustrate the role of perception and coping with stress. They are not always bad, but there is a fine line between 'unhealthy' and 'healthy' illusions. They can be 'healthy' if they maintain your self-esteem and optimism about coping with stress – for example, if they allow you not to become overwhelmed by stress so that you can argue 'So what?' or 'I can do something about it!' They become 'unhealthy' when they interfere with your 'reality testing' – that is, your ability to evaluate your stress objectively and to objectively differentiate between your external and internal worlds. If you engage in falsification of reality (by using massive denial, for example), it could indicate poor coping and lead to more stress. Other examples when illusions become destructive are:

- when you fail to see that alcohol or drug use is harming you;
- when you have the illusion that you are invulnerable and believe 'it won't happen to me';
- if you fail to see your limitations and continue to strive way beyond your abilities;
- if you ignore the symptoms of stress or physical warning signs that might place your health in jeopardy; or
- if you can't make the perceptual shifts to see more effective alternatives to cope with stress.

Since so many factors affect the way you construct your perceptual world, the evidence of your senses is not always reliable. There are those times when seeing is not believing or when seeing is misleading. Although we are concerned with real life perceptions in this book, the illustrations used in this section show how ambiguous perception can be. The same is true when you apply your perception to interpreting your wider knowledge of the world – especially the stressors in it.

There are other concepts in perception such as perceptual constancy, wherein the relationship of the object to its background remains the same. In this type of perception seeing is believing. That is, your world remains stable despite great changes in sensory input. For example, you will perceive a car as a car whether you are driving it, overtaking it or looking at it from a distance. There are numerous similar experiences in your daily life where the actual visual stimulus changes, but your perception of what you see stays constant. Even if you see it from different angles, colours and shapes, your perception of it will stay constant.

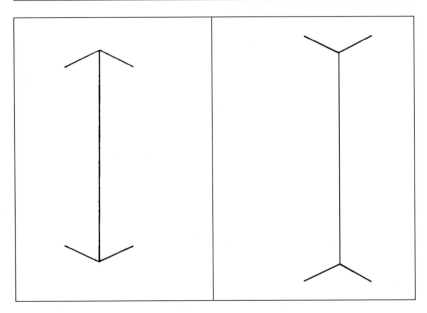

FIGURE 7.6   *Perceptual illusions.* This is known as the Müller-Lyer illusion. Which line is longer? Most people say it is the one on the right, but they are the same length.

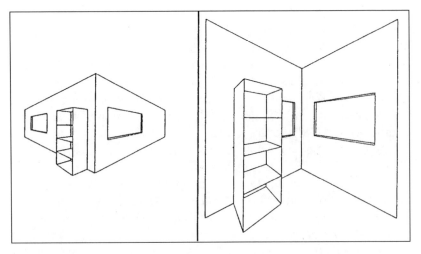

FIGURE 7.7   The same illusion illustrated in Figure 7.6 can be seen in this example of how we create our perceptions.

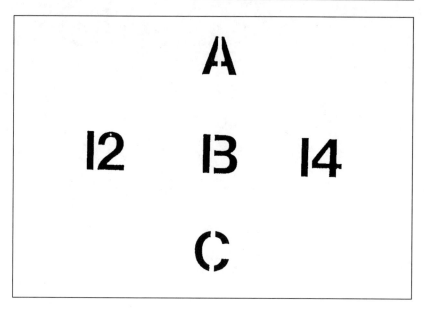

FIGURE 7.8 *The figure in the centre is ambiguous. You can see it either as a B or as the number 13.*

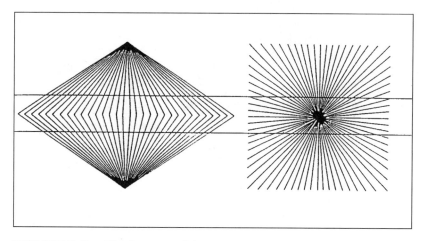

FIGURE 7.9 *The horizontal lines are parallel, although it may not seem so at first glance.*

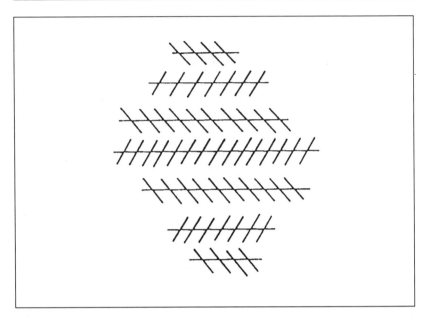

FIGURE 7.10   *It is hard to believe, but the horizontal lines are parallel.*

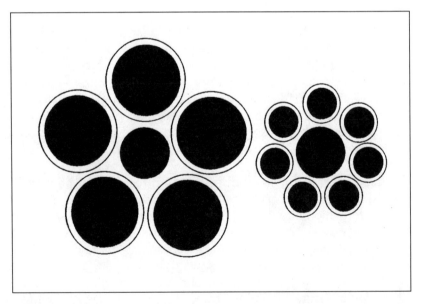

FIGURE 7.11   *Do the circles in the centre seem the same size?*

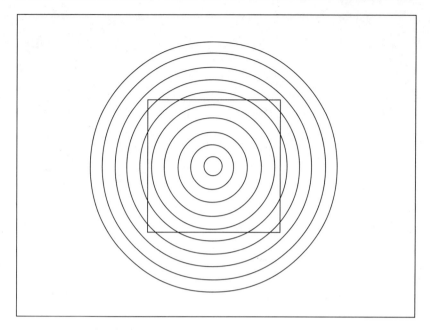

FIGURE 7.12 *Does the square have straight lines?*

Perceptual defence is another concept which illustrates how your perception is affected by unconscious feelings. It happens when you take longer to recognise offensive or threatening stimuli than you would take to recognise neutral ones. Another example where un-conscious feelings can affect perception is the meaning you attach to a specific word, such as to the make, model or even colour of a certain car. This is especially so if it involves emotionally loaded words which are more quickly identified than neutral ones. Because percep-tion is creative and it does not reveal a literal version of reality to you, but rather something you create of what you perceive, it is also influenced by your perceptual habits and styles. These are in turn influenced by your experiences and various psychological states or moods.

Other concepts in this regard are pattern recognition, perceptual set and the perceptual cycle. Pattern recognition is how we structure visual information into meaningful shapes. In reading road signs, for example, you not only interpret certain non-verbal signs to provide you with information, but you also recognise patterns made by letters or words and even whole sets of words. The ability to recognise patterns like this in life is basic to coherent perception. Look at the illustration in Figure 7.13 of the same characters in different scripts. Despite the differences, you still recognise the letters.

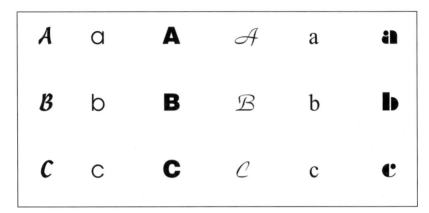

FIGURE 7.13 *Similar characters in different scripts.* We tend to recognise the same characters or shapes even if they are different, for example, in reading.

We have seen that attention plays a role in perception. Since we are continually bombarded with information that we have to make sense of, and there is usually more information than we can take in at any one moment, we tend to select what we want to see and pay attention to it. This we do by focusing our perception so that we selectively perceive some things rather than others. We put our perception in a state of readiness to do this, and this is referred to as perceptual set. Here, the word 'set' means the same as in 'Ready, set, go' as used in the start of a race, for example. Your perceptual set is personal: your psychological states, motives and personality characteristics will influence what and how you perceive. Even social pressures can influence your perceptual set.

The essence of the perceptual cycle, on the other hand, involves the fact that we are continuously and actively involved in constructing a dynamic understanding of our world: one that changes all the time. We don't create a one off, static representation of our world. Because of this, perception changes all the time and no two perceptual acts are really ever precisely the same in every way. Some people even claim that their perception goes beyond the normal senses, such as in extra sensory perception (which refers to paranormal abilities) and in clairvoyance, telepathy, out-of-body experiences and precognition (the perception of events that have not happened yet). Another type of perception includes hallucinations or false perceptions where the person might, for example, regard an image as a real sensory experience when there is no actual sensory stimulus. These are usually associated with severe psychological disorders, such as in schizophrenia. These are perhaps the most extreme examples of how psychological states can affect perception.

We come into the world with other 'factory installed wiring' that help us to survive. Examples are 'top-down' and 'bottom-up' perception or information processing. In a sense, the one is the opposite of the other. In 'top-down' information processing we emphasise the importance of prior knowledge. 'Top-down' events originate in our thoughts and the brain interprets them as messages which are sent throughout the body, signalling it to respond. In 'bottom-up' information processing we depend on current information. A typical computer, for example, processes information using the 'bottom-up' approach. Unlike humans, it cannot process information where later considerations affect earlier ones, because computers have no controlling 'executive ability' that can modify previous or later experience. Humans do, however, have such executive abilities or functions. These consist of those capacities that enable them to successfully engage in independent purposeful and self-serving behaviour. In this sense, executive functions differ from our intellectual functions, although the two are interdependent. For example, questions about executive functions relate to how or whether a person does something, whereas questions about intellectual functions relate to 'how to' and 'what or how much' the person does.

In summary, your perceptions can contribute to appropriate interpretation of your environment, or to misinterpretation that causes you stress. Moreover, research has shown that you are linked to what you perceive because of your own activities. Your perception is influenced by the possibility of a range of actions that you might take. For example, you wouldn't just perceive a car as a vehicle for transport to work when you buy it, but also for other potential uses like fun or boosting social status, for example. An important point to remember in coping with stress, is that your perception can be affected by various psychological influences such as your psychological state, needs, culture, beliefs, values, attitudes, expectations, emotions and thoughts.

Thoughts

On average you think about 50 000 thoughts a day. Thoughts can be pleasant or unpleasant. You can use them to imagine good and bad, to produce stress or to minimise it. For example, reliving unpleasant memories can fill your present and future with apprehension and stress. Whereas such stress-producing thoughts can have a negative effect on you, pleasant and positive thoughts can have a stress-reducing effect on you, be beneficial and produce a sense of well-being. Your thoughts can affect both your emotions and behaviour.

Your perceptions result in thoughts. From these you make up your 'frame of reference', 'cognitive map' or 'thought map'. This is your guide through the complexities of life and includes your views of who you are, what is important to you and how stress impacts on you. This thought shapes your decisions, emotions and behaviour. You often assume you perceive things the way they are, and this misperception leads to stress. You might not take into consideration that there may be other interpretations and thoughts about the same things that could be less stress-producing. For example, what do you understand by the word 'knowing'? You might say that you know a lot about your car and how to drive it, and that you know driving it to work causes you stress. Somebody else, however, might have a different opinion about stress and driving to work depending on that person's perception and thoughts about it, for example. Most authorities would argue that knowing involves committing something to memory but that it also involves the 'how-to' part of you, that is, your thoughts. To cope with stress, therefore, you need to change any stress-producing thoughts to stress-reducing ones – just as you have to do with perception.

Thoughts can also be organised into thinking strategies which can be used by you to understand yourself and your environment. But just as with perception, they can be used by you to make your life more difficult. For example, a stressed person uses a thinking strategy that persistently focuses on negative rather than positive thoughts. Such a person ends up being negatively conditioned, which produces more stressful behaviour and poorer stress management skills. In this book the use of a thinking strategy called cognitive restructuring or thought changing is used as an important part of coping with stress. Thought changing involves a number of different psychological techniques based on the principle of changing emotions and behaviour by correcting distorted thinking. Basic to this is the view that emotions and feelings begin with a core thought or belief. If the thought is irrational or dysfunctional and causes stress, it will lead to similar emotions and behaviour. So, to change the upsetting emotions and behaviour into more functional ones that don't produce negative stress, the original thought must be changed to counter your stress response. By practising this, you learn how to progressively eliminate negative conditioning caused by negative thoughts and replace them with positive thoughts.

The essential message here is: effective stress management also embodies identifying and changing negative thoughts that result in thinking errors which cause stress, correcting such thinking errors and cultivating a problem-solving (stress-reducing) rather than a problem-creating (stress-inducing) mode of thinking.

Emotions

Emotions can be considered as contributing to an enrichment of experience and as safeguards of survival. They are not static but are events or reactions which continually change and have many functions in life, such as permitting you to establish close bonds, get help from others, etc. They also serve to warn you of problems. Sometimes emotions get out of control and are not in your best interests. They can include universally felt primary emotions that all people have which are part of your evolutionary heritage, and secondary emotions which are culturally influenced and are specific to certain cultures. That is, cultural influences that you have been and are exposed to can also affect the experience and expression of your emotions. Emotions are not the same as feelings although the two go hand in hand. Feelings are what you experience as a result of your emotions. People think they might intuitively understand what they mean by the term emotion, but most psychologists agree that emotions are complex and have both a physiological and a thought-based component. Furthermore, emotional memory is an important aspect of what you remember. Emotional memory is not always stored in the brain as facts, but rather as emotions associated with certain things that happen to you. In a way we tend to express emotions physically but in fact use them psychosocially. For example, should there be damage to the amygdala (two almond-shaped structures) in the limbic system which is the emotional control centre (see Figure 2.4), emotions can be severely affected. A recent example reported a case of a woman whose ability to perceive danger was impaired due to damage to her amygdala. Emotions are often seen as the heart and soul of human existence, and one of the most obvious places to look for emotion is in facial expression. The famous researcher on evolution, Charles Darwin, wrote about this in his classical book *The Expression of the Emotions in Man and Animals* (as long ago as the 1870s). Humans are social beings and many of our emotions involve other people. We need to communicate our wishes, desires and motives to others, and facial expressions serve this purpose *par excellence*.

Although emotions depend on a complex combination of physiological and psychological factors, they also have a lot to do with your perceptions. This is so because the type of emotion you feel often depends on your perception and interpretation of what is happening to you, which in turn affects your thoughts about it, as we saw earlier. That is, emotions are influenced by both the explanations and interpretation you provide to yourself based on your perceptions, and by your resultant thought patterns. In this way an experience is not always stored in your brain as a fact, but as an emotion (that is, as an emotional memory). Emotions and emotional memories in turn affect your behaviour and your stress response. They can also vary in degree and intensity, such as when you make a distinction between worry and terror, sadness and depression, etc. These distinctions also relate to the intensity of your feelings resulting from a particularly stressful situation.

The English language contains several hundred different words describing emotions and feelings, but it seems unlikely that we actually experience this many and some represent only very subtle nuances or shadings of mood. The universal emotions we all experience consist of a set of basic or primary emotions including: love, anger, joy, sadness, surprise and fear. Emotions can be positive (pleasant) and negative (unpleasant). You might think that positive and negative emotions are opposites. This is not always the case, as people can experience both negative and positive emotions simultaneously. Research on brain activity during emotional states indicates that positive emotions tend to be processed in the left hemisphere of the cerebral cortex, while negative emotions tend to be processed in the right hemisphere. This explains why positive and negative emotions, such as happiness and sadness, can sometimes be felt at the same time. This is important for stress management, considering the specialised functions of the two hemispheres of the brain and because negative emotions differ from positive ones in the types of perceptions and thought patterns that generate them.

Research has shown that the emotional repertoire of humans grows steadily richer during early development. For example, newborn babies enter the world with a small array of emotional expressions, including surprise, distress and pleasure or joy. Generally, anger becomes visible at four months and after six months new expressions of emotion, such as fear and shyness, appear. More complex emotions such as empathy, guilt, embarrassment, shame and pride appear later as the child gains an awareness of social standards and a more sophisticated self-concept. As we have seen, culture is important in emotions. The culture in which the child grows up will affect emotional display, and most communities and societies have 'display rules' that prescribe to their members how and when emotions can and should be expressed, even when at work. To complicate matters further, often human beings do not express their emotions openly and may even convey them indirectly through, for example, non-verbal signals such as body language. Even the absence of movement can have significant meaning in terms of body language. This is discussed further in Chapter 12.

Furthermore, people generally hold strong views about the differences in expression of emotions between men and women which are also influenced by culture. There is little scientific evidence that the one sex feels emotions more intensely or more often than the other if they are from the same cultural background. But there is some evidence that the sexes differ in the expression of their emotions, especially in Western cultures. For example, men tend to express anger towards strangers more frequently than women when their perception is that they have been challenged, especially by other men. They also tend to express anger and fear more aggressively, especially if they feel their pride is hurt, and they might be more aggressive when they want to demonstrate or establish their dominance or simply get their way. On the other hand, women are likely to be considered more emotional, not because they necessarily are, but because of their perceived sensitivity to emotions, especially in other people. They are more likely to express emotions such as sadness, loneliness and embarrassment, and to share these with close friends and family. Most men might consider these emotions 'not macho'. When stressed, men tend to withdraw to brood about it, focus on resolving it alone or conversely do things to forget about it like engaging in competitive behaviour, racing their cars, etc. Women, on the other hand, tend to talk it through with a trusted person and feel less inclined to be embarrassed by their feelings. This could also explain why many psychotherapists report that they see more women in psychotherapy than men. Not because women have more problems, but because they are prepared to talk about them more readily.

Psychologists have recently focused on a different form of intellectual expression called emotional intelligence. What we usually understand under the traditional concept of IQ or intelligence quotient seems to contribute only about 20 per cent of what we need for success. The rest comes from other factors, including emotional intelligence. Emotional intelligence consists of various aspects, including self-awareness, zeal and persistence, self-control, self-motivation and impulse control. These skills can be taught and result in good 'people skills'. The essence of emotional intelligence involves a sense of self-regulation and the ability to delay impulses or instant gratification in favour of satisfying a longer-term goal. When you are faced with immediate temptation and you can remind yourself of your long-term goals and not give into the need for instant gratification, you obviously have a higher emotional intelligence than if you give in to the temptation immediately and forsake the long-term goals. The ability to recognise feelings as they occur is another keystone of emotional intelligence, as is the ability to motivate yourself positively and the capacity to know how others feel. The importance of this for good interpersonal skills is obvious – the more skillful a person is at discerning the feelings behind another person's signals, the better that person can control the signals he or she sends.

Research in psychology has repeatedly stressed the importance of perception, thoughts, beliefs and needs in determining our motives and behaviour. You might be familiar with Abraham Maslow's theory of motivation and hierarchy of needs, illustrated in Figure 7.14. Supposedly, needs at the bottom must be satisfied before needs at the top. The particular order is only an approximation of how people attend to their various needs. Inherent to this idea is the notion that people's needs and motives are interconnected, and that satisfying one need will depend on the current status of the others. In addition, when we need something or have an interest in it, we are more likely to let it influence our perceptions and our thoughts. There is also an explicit connection between emotions, needs and motivation because emotions tend to amplify our drives, which play an important role in our behaviour.

All these issues regarding emotions have obvious implications for stress management. We have to learn to control our negative and stress-related emotions in order to overcome stress. Fundamental questions here are: 'Are you in control of your emotions, or do they control you?' and 'Do you use your emotions to justify your stress-related behaviour?' Remember, it is not the raw material of what you see that creates your emotions – your brain creates them.

Behaviour

Popular writing and folklore have historically portrayed the heart as the seat of emotions, and the brain as the seat of rational thought. However, even though emotions might result in a quicker heartbeat or an 'aching' heart and we talk about 'what the eye doesn't see, the heart doesn't grieve over', it is more complicated than this. A web of signals are implicated that travel back and forth on nerve and brain pathways which are involved in a complex circuitry and which influences behaviour.

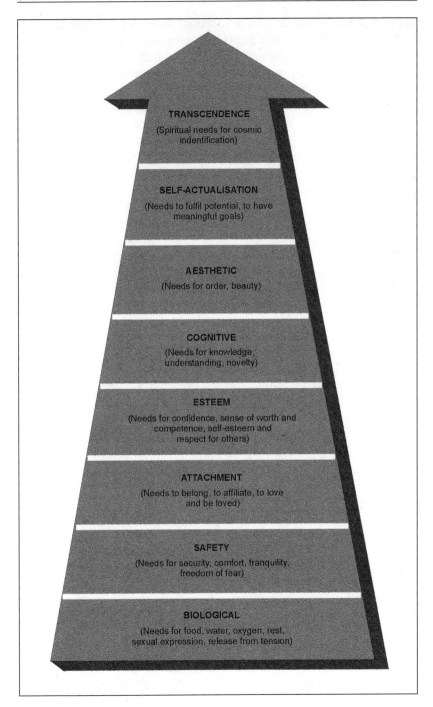

FIGURE 7.14 *Maslow's hierarchy of needs.*

In this way, behaviour involves your total response to a situation. It includes your actions and reactions as observed by others, as well as the behaviour of the organs and cells in your body. Your central nervous system is the very bedrock of behaviour. In this process the brain influences behaviour, but behaviour also influences the brain. Not only your visible behaviour, but also the behaviour of organs and cells in your body are affected by your perceptions, thoughts, emotions and a wide variety of factors, including stress. This is the link between stress and disease. Rather, human behaviour (or misbehaviour) is at the root of most of what is wrong in our society. Whereas the 1990s were subject to an intense research focus on neuroscience in the 'Decade of the Brain', it is likely that the early part of the 2000s will see a more intense focus on addressing the underpinnings of behaviour to ensure answers to society's most daunting challenges. The 'Decade of Behaviour' might become a new research cornerstone in stress management and health.

YOU ARE NOT A PASSIVE VICTIM

How does all this tie together in stress management? You can decrease stress by changing your perceptions and thinking, which will lead to different emotions, feelings and behaviour. That is, you can learn to cope with stress or reduce it. How you perceive the stressors in your life can affect the intensity of your feelings which result from your emotions. Although most psychologists agree that emotions are different from perceptions and thoughts, our emotions interact closely with these functions. Emotions may initially be aroused automatically but the next step involves how the mind reacts. This reaction is influenced by perception, thinking processes and other functions such as memory. Memories of past experiences can sometimes be as powerful in arousing emotions and influencing behaviour as stressful events themselves. There are occasions when emotions and feelings seem to lead to a fast response, so quick that you're sure you feel before you think. However, there is substantial psychological evidence that in many instances thinking can precede emotions and that you can change your thinking to improve how you feel, thereby altering your behaviour.

Unlike cameras, humans care about what they see. The more you regard events as stressful and difficult to control, the more conflicts you experience about them, the more you blame yourself and feel powerless to change, and the more stress you experience. You end up in a vicious cycle, one which renders you helpless to cope with stress. The key to effective stress control is to change your perception, which

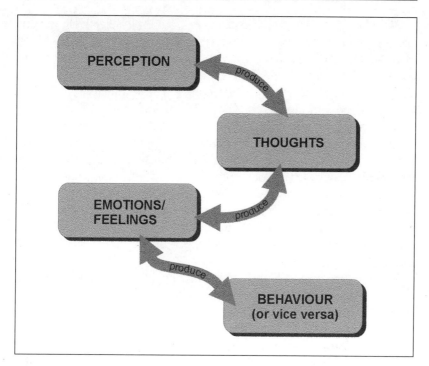

FIGURE 7.15

affects how you think about the stress: that way your feelings, behaviour and your response to stress can change (Figure 7.15). In effect, you have to change yourself by changing your perception. In other words, when you make a perceptual shift regarding your interpretation of the stress in your life, you will change in the way you look at and interpret things. You will stop making catastrophes out of minor disappointments. It is a bit like changing your psychological lenses or looking glasses so that you see the world from a different perspective.

Let's focus on an innovative approach to such 'thought changing', one which originated from the technique of 'perceptual shifting' – a method of changing not just isolated thoughts, but the general pattern of your thinking. That is, perceptual patterns and cognitive schemata (whole thinking patterns) sometimes need to be changed. Remember, different people will respond differently to the same situation and more often than not, stress can result from mistaken perceptions that might even have their roots in earlier experiences. Often these earlier experiences lead to further mistaken perceptions, which are not corrected during the normal processes of growing up and maturing.

What happens is that as you grow up, your brain selectively screens and interprets data which is then formed into thinking patterns. Many of these thinking patterns are taught to you by significant people in your life, and the more they are repeated, the stronger they become and the more difficult they are to change. These thinking patterns in turn produce emotional and behavioural responses. If these responses are negative, such as producing negative stress and you want to change them, you have to change the perceptual and thinking patterns that elicit them in the first place. Sometimes this also means identifying a mistake in your philosophy of life and seeking a more valid and fulfilling one. The idea is to produce a shift in your perceptions by changing them from stress-producing ones to stress-reducing ones, and to remove conflict between what are realistic and what are mistaken perceptions in order to produce whole patterns of positive thoughts, emotions and behaviour.

Take an example of you slowly driving in traffic when another driver suddenly cuts in front of you. Based on earlier experiences, your perception of the situation would influence your thinking patterns and subsequent emotional and behavioural responses to the situation. You could perceive it as an effort by a rude or impatient driver to cut you off, producing all sorts of 'nasty' thoughts about the driver (including negative emotions such as anger), resulting in behavioural responses that could make the situation worse and increase your stress levels. Or you could change that perception and perceive it as the other driver's effort to avoid being caught in a potential accident situation. This would result in different thinking patterns, for example that he or she had no other choice to avoid an accident, that some drivers are actually not that bad, and that you are lucky there wasn't an accident, which will produce positive emotional and behavioural responses in you and less stress.

When you are in a stressful situation, consider how another person would interpret and feel it. Then try and work out how many people (for example, out of 10) you know who would see it differently and feel different. This is a crucial exercise, because you might think your way of looking at the situation is the only way. But if it produces stress in you, think about how less stressed people in the same situation would be looking at it. Isn't it more realistic for you to start changing how you look at it and be more in line with those who are less stressed? I am not saying 'be like everyone else', just allow yourself the freedom from stress some people have mastered.

Perceptual shifts can occur more rapidly if you aim for the 'aha' experience. That is, you suddenly develop insight into why you need to change your perception and you can see the benefits for you. It is almost as if your internal 'psychological light' has suddenly been turned on. This is made easier if you accept that the current damaging perception is harmful to you and causing you stress, and that there is an acceptable alternative perception that will cause less stress. If you feel that you are trapped by your old perception, your one escape route is to accept the new one which will reduce the stress. You are ready to make the shift when the old one causes you unbearable stress and you are convinced that the new perception is the way out. This is important because you will soon learn that you tend to change more readily when you have to. The pressure of necessity is something that has evolved in human beings. When the going gets tough, change! Also, you will realise that new information is learnt more readily following your new perception, if the new information is associated with facts that you have already stored in your memory.

Try the exercise in Figure 7.16 to help you gain a better understanding of the nature of making a perceptual shift. This is called a transposing technique in which some people will see an old woman and others a young woman – that is, different people will respond differently to the same stimulus.

A useful way to encourage yourself to make perceptual shifts in order to reduce stress is to keep a perceptual shift record. You can use this exercise to test whether your stress-producing perceptions are true or not. Ask yourself two basic questions: 'How true is my perception?' and 'What can I do about it?' You can look for evidence to support it, and for alternatives that argue against it that are less stress-producing. Think it through carefully. Meditate on experiences that prove your negative perceptions. Don't forget to date your exercise so you can monitor how your perceptions change with time. Your perceptual shift record could look like the one illustrated in Table 7.1. This type of exercise will also help you change your internal dialogue or self-talk from a negative to a positive one, as discussed more fully in Chapter 14.

Remember, you have many cognitive templates or thinking programmes which developed as you grew up. You use these to interpret what is happening to you in different ways and frequently don't question their accuracy. If they were incorrect or faulty to start with, a long history of dysfunctional thinking can eventually result in maladaptive thinking programmes. They can become so potent that your brain persistently selects them for the same interpretation of events no matter how inappropriate or dysfunctional they are to your present situation. When your brain scans for information, it receives,

Source: Originally *Puck*
6 November 1915

**FIGURE 7.16   *A transposing technique using a reversible
picture to help with changing your perception.*** *On a sheet of
blank paper make a list on the left side of all the details of your old
perceptions. On the right side change the details of the old
perceptions into new, more positive perceptions. Use the above
picture as an example to do this, in which the old perception is one
of an old lady and the new perception is of a young woman (that is,
the whole 'gestalt' or total theme). Your lists could like like this, in
which you should practise each detail of the total theme until the
old one fades and you see the new one automatically.*

Old perceptions (old woman)	New perceptions (young woman)
tip of the nose	tip of chin
eye	ear
mouth	neck band
wart on nose	nose
hair on nose	eyelash
chin	lower neck
looking at you	looking away from you

TABLE 7.1

	PERCEPTUAL SHIFT RECORD		
DATE	INITIAL NEGATIVE PERCEPTION	WHAT IS THE EVIDENCE FOR THIS PERCEPTION	ALTERNATIVE POSITIVE PERCEPTION	CHALLENGE THE NEGATIVE PERCEPTION (OUTCOME)
?	Write down the original negative perception that caused the stress.	Write down the evidence you have to support whether this negative perception is true or not.	Write down an alternative, positive perception that is less stress-producing. Your best argument against the negative perception.	Spend some time meditating whether you have disproved the original, stress-producing perception and answer yes or no. Is it false or true?
?	**Example 1** I am useless = negative perception. **Outcome** Negative thoughts, emotions and behaviour = more stress, anxiety or depression.	I had a silly accident and damaged my car. I can't drive properly.	This is my first accident after many years of safe driving. No one was injured, I have learnt from it = positive perception. **Outcome** Positive thoughts, emotions and behaviour = less stress, anxiety or depression.	Yes, I have disproved the first perception. It is false. I am not a useless driver. This was simply an accident which I can avoid in future. I can be a safe driver. **Outcome** Positive response, positive feelings. Less stress.
?	**Example 2** I'm a failure, I might as well give up. There is no hope for me = negative perception. **Outcome** Negative thoughts, emotions and behaviour = more stress, anxiety or depression.	I can't reach my sales target this month. It doesn't matter how hard I try.	I have reached my sales targets before. I can do it again. What can I do to manage my time better? = positive perception. **Outcome** Positive thoughts, emotions and behaviour = less stress, anxiety or depression.	Yes, I have disproved the first perception. It is false. I am not a failure. I can succeed. This is a temporary setback. I can avoid getting into this situation again. **Outcome** Positive response, positive feelings. Less stress.

looks for and selects those thinking programmes that are compatible with perceptions you already have (pre-existing ones). These are then woven into a current thought pattern that matches and suits what you already think you perceive. If your pre-existing perceptions and thoughts were negative, they in turn influence you to see aspects of your present world as stressors – not because they really are, but because they reflect what you are seeing and thinking, which are now based on your re-inforced negative perceptions and thinking patterns that cause stress. Why? Because you (like most people) tend to want to see the world the way you want to see it, and because you are locked into those old thinking programmes. It acts as a negative cycle of perceiving and thinking about your world. In this process you are often closed to alternative perceptions, thereby either engaging in misinterpretations or denying yourself a different, larger and perhaps more accurate picture. What you need to do is take into account the many different perceptions and ways that a potential stressor can be viewed and interpreted, so that you develop different, more positive thinking patterns about it that will lead to a healthier internal dialogue.

CONCLUSION

In order to deal with the stress associated with a particular perceptual stance, an alternative, less stress-inducing perception is necessary. This will help you to change your thinking and internal dialogue as well as your emotions and behaviour from negative to positive ones. Not only does this embody a re-appraisal of the stressor, but it also allows you to recognise your own misinterpretations and to appreciate the value of looking at your stressors through different lenses. You can look at a glass that is half filled with water as either half empty or half full. The choice is yours. Looking at it as half full carries a more positive message. You can of course look at it in yet another way – a third perspective according to which there are no absolute measures of emptiness or fullness, leaving you with endless possibilities.

Many traditional therapies in stress management focus on talking therapy. Simply talking about stress is not enough. Just as you won't learn to drive your car safely by only talking about it, you won't manage your stress just by talking about it. You need to acquire the appropriate experience and skills. This also takes practise. The more you practise at changing your perception, the better you get at it. If you want to be a skilled driver, you have to practise. If you want to be healthy and physically fit, you engage in living a healthy lifestyle and getting regular physical exercise. Likewise, you have to do the necessary psychological and mental exercises to get your mind healthy and fit to deal with stress – and continue to do them. You have to do this regularly – until it becomes part of your normal lifestyle. You might think that you cannot achieve this. This is not true. Changing your perception is a skill that can be learned, just as exercise or relaxation techniques can be learned. If you want to deal with stress, you have to practise changing your perception. This will help you transform failure into success and avoid what has been called psychosclerosis – a hardening of attitude which is not only stressful but can be damaging to your psychological well-being. Other guidelines of what to practise are provided in the rest of this book. Remember the maxim 'practise makes perfect' when you read on.

SUMMARY OF THE MAIN PRINCIPLES

- Change yourself to achieve psychological self-empowerment.
- There are always different ways of looking at the same problem. This involves perception.
- Nothing is stressful, unless you interpret it as such.
- Perception is a psychological function that helps you to organise and interpret stimuli from your environment – the way you look at things.
- Perception influences your thoughts and thinking processes (cognitions).
- Thoughts can be pleasant or unpleasant, negative or positive, stress-producing or stress-reducing.
- Thoughts are organised into thought maps and thinking strategies which you use to understand yourself and your environment. They affect emotions.
- Emotions serve many psychosocial functions.
- There are universally felt primary emotions that occur in all cultures and secondary emotions which are specific to certain cultures.
- You experience feelings as a result of your emotions.
- Emotions can be both negative and positive. They affect behaviour.
- Your emotional intelligence is an important factor in coping successfully.
- Behaviour involves your total response to a situation.
- How you perceive things, therefore, will affect your thoughts, emotions and behaviour.
- A basic step to cope with stress is to change your perception about the stressor, which will change your thinking about it, how you feel about it and ultimately your behaviour and stress response.
- When you perceive a situation as controllable, it becomes an important part of your feelings of security and psychological self-empowerment. You need to make a basic perceptual shift to do so.

CHAPTER 8

Think flow not flood

THE 'FLOOD-OR-FLOW' RESPONSE

WILLIAM JAMES, a 19th century philosopher, said: 'Whilst part of what we perceive comes through our senses from the objects before us, another part (and it may be the larger part) always comes out of our own head.'

The concept of 'flood-or-flow', developed during my research on stress, has to do with harnessing your formidable mind power to control the rising tide of your psychological response to stress, and going with the flow of events rather than permitting them to flood you. You want to get the energy of your emotions to work for you rather than against you. If you think 'flow' and not 'flood' when confronted with stress and make that perceptual shift to change the way you see and think about stressful events, you can go with their flow and view them as challenges you can swim through rather than events that will drown you. The key to this is to maintain a proper perspective on the perceived stressful situation, and to cultivate the

FIGURE 8.1 *The way you look at it (your perception) will affect your response.*

characteristics of the flow response listed in Table 8.1. Start by considering these two questions: 'Is it really a stressor, or is it a lie?' (see Figure 8.1) and 'What will this matter in a week, a month or a year's time?' Once you've addressed these, you'll see that what you consider to be so stressful that it overwhelms you today, might not be a problem at all sometime in the future.

TABLE 8.1

THE 'FLOOD-OR-FLOW' RESPONSE	
CHARACTERISTICS OF THE 'FLOW' RESPONSE	CHARACTERISTICS OF THE 'FLOOD' RESPONSE
The 'flow' person is: • assertive • progressive • on the move/mobile • current • original • successful • adaptable • easy-going • fluid/flexible/tolerant • open • optimistic • receptive • versatile	The 'flood' person is: • non-assertive • easily crowded • easily flushed • prone to outbursts/aggressiveness • rash • easily swamped/overwhelmed • given to excesses • pessimistic • inflexible/intolerant • obstinate • rigid • stubborn • opinionated
Such a person: • rises to challenges • has high self-worth • sheds emotional baggage • has an appropriate mission statement	Such a person: • avoids challenges • carries emotional baggage • has low self-worth • lacks an appropriate mission statement

The 'flood-or-flow' response can be construed as a psychological response when compared to the 'fight-or-flight' response, which is a physiological response to stress. The 'fight-or-flight' response is designed to assist you to cope physically with danger. This danger of course can be figurative as well as actual and your response begins with the perception of a threat, whatever that might be for you. The 'flood-or-flow' response can help you cope with the psychological aspects of that threat and the resultant stress.

When an emergency physical action is demanded from the threatening situation, excellent back-up support is automatically provided by your body. But if the stress is prolonged, you can become weakened, age more rapidly and become more susceptible to physical or psychological disorders. If you experience continued stress, you live in a constant state of readiness to respond to the 'fight-or-flight' action. In a way the fight manoeuvres are based on the perception that the best form of defence is attack, whereas the use of psychological defence mechanisms are flight manoeuvres.

The negative stress response is like a small amount of snow which gets dislodged high up on the slopes of a snow-covered mountain. As it descends it picks up more snow (stress), gathers momentum, surges along out of control and eventually turns into an avalanche that swallows you up in its wake – that is, if you don't take preventative steps to get out of its path or control the process in the first place. From a psychological perspective you are now flooded with the stress. You need to prevent this flooding and rather go with the flow of events, which will give you the time to put into practice some of the other stress management skills discussed in this book. It's a bit like a reed in a river bed. The reed that is inflexible and resists bending with the flood of water caused by the storm or flash flood higher up the river will snap. The reed that bends with the flow rises again and survives once the flood is past, as in the adage 'better bend than break' (Figure 8.2). By its very nature then, the 'flow' part of the 'flood-or-flow' response embodies the issues discussed in the previous chapter, especially making the required perceptual shift and obtaining a different perspective.

BOUNCE BACK
Implicit in the concept of 'flowing' is the ability to go with the flow (Figure 8.2) and to cultivate the characteristics listed in Table 8.1, as well as the ability to bounce back. If you can't avoid change or stress in your life, you can change how you perceive it and flow with it, so that you can give yourself the opportunity to bounce back.

YOUR 'INNER EYE'
Perception is a function used to interpret and make sense of your world, and that perception is in the eye of the beholder. That is, your brain does not respond blindly, but uses its 'inner eye' to exercise its own interpretation of what you perceive. This might be very different from other people's perception. Perception helps you receive and process information about your environment. It is represented by your six senses, but also by your greater non-physical world expressed by

FIGURE 8.2   *Think flow not flood.* *The person who can learn to be more flexible and flow with events that cause stress, will be better able to cope than the person who is inflexible.*

other aspects of you. Psychologists observed long ago that humans have a tendency to perceive that which they expect, hope or fear to see, which is associated with a type of 'displaced perception'. Some psychologists find this useful to study when they analyse or interpret their patients' projective psychological test responses, such as those obtained from the inkblot test, story-telling techniques or drawings. They search for clues when the person displaces perception in their responses to the tests. Past experiences influence those responses. Freud himself assumed that memories of percepts (objects perceived by the senses) influence perception of contemporary stimuli.

We now know (from modern work on stress) that if a situation is perceived as stressful, it usually becomes highly stressful, especially if you also think (and believe) that your resources to cope are inadequate. Whether they are or not doesn't matter. What you think they are, they will be. Sometimes in your attempts to make sense of your world, you can misinterpret reality. Stress is often about such misinterpretations of what is happening to you. Because stress can be such a subjective and personal experience, it starts with your perception of the stressor in your life.

But stress is also about your inflexibility to accept change – the inability to flow. To prevent yourself from being flooded by stress, it is important to remember that there is more to what you see than your senses observe. Take vision, for example. Although your eyes perceive two-dimensional images on the screen of the retina, your perception is actually three-dimensional. The images of each eye not only provide you with clues as to the size, colour, shadow, etc. of what you see, but because they observe the images you see from two slightly different angles (two different eyes), you see two slightly different versions of the same image. Your brain fuses them into a single three-dimensional image which you interpret to make sense to you. You can use this interpretation to flow with events or you can drown in the flood of your own perception.

Although everyone uses perception to interpret what is stressful and what isn't and has resultant thoughts and emotions that influence behaviour, not everyone will develop a stress-related disorder. But, it is likely that everyone will at various times experience anger, elation, envy, grief, sadness, fear, difficulties with eating or sleeping, problems in life and relationships, etc. These are the things that make up the very essence of life. Whether they will flood you depends largely on your perception of the stress associated with them and your ability to flow with the changes they bring.

In the early days of psychology it was believed that our images of our external world were a tapestry of sensations and that studying these sensations would unlock our psychological world. We now know that we do not simply 'sense' our world, but that we also interpret it according to the way we perceive it by using our 'inner eye'. In this process, even a simple image (or stimulus) can be misinterpreted to cause stress.

Perception is not a passive process, but is active and constructive, sometimes imaginative, sometimes logical, sometimes illogical and sometimes plainly wrong. Various factors can influence the images or scenes as perceived by your 'inner eye'. We saw, for example, that what you perceive can be influenced by your expectations, past experiences, personality, your current needs, beliefs, thoughts and emotions. All this in turn will affect your ability to adapt and to be flexible so that you can flow with events to minimise stress.

UNCONSCIOUS FEELINGS

The ability to flow is implicitly linked to many aspects of your perception which can even occur outside of your awareness, because your perception is also coloured by your unconscious feelings and basic needs. Because people construct their inner world through experiences, unconscious feelings and basic needs are particularly important in perception. Your psychological equilibrium is partly determined by your perception of how such 'hidden' factors in your life influence your ability to flow with events.

The upshot of all this is that we invariably go through life unaware of the subtlety and range of our perception and how this impacts on our ability to flow with events that are potential stressors. We perceive more than we realise, despite only needing a fraction of this information to function.

YOUR SELF-PERCEPTION

Perception is also influenced by self-perception – that is, the way we see ourselves and the basic sense that we make of ourselves in relation to our world. You're probably familiar with coined terms like self-worth and self-esteem. These are factors that play an important role in flowing with stress.

In addition to the aforesaid, you can use the same basic approaches discussed in Table 7.1 to test your perception of potential causes of stress so that you are not flooded by it. Ask yourself these questions: 'How true is my self-perception?' 'How true is my perception of the stressor and its cause?' and 'What can I do about it?'

YOUR PSYCHOLOGICAL BRAKE

To find the answers and to prevent flooding, you might require a bit of time to carefully assess or re-assess a situation and then proceed slowly, gradually and cautiously. Let's use another memory aid to assist with this. We all know that a wasp is a striped, stinging insect resembling a bee. Imagine the stressor as the wasp. You don't want it to sting you, so you don't want to stir up the wasp. We talk about being waspish (being irritable, snappish, ill-tempered, cantankerous, grumpy, fretful, etc. – all signs of stress). An easy and useful technique to prevent being flooded by stress, is to use the memory aid A WASP whenever you are confronted with potential stress.

A → APPLY YOUR PSYCHOLOGICAL BRAKE
W → WAIT WHILE YOU
A → ASSESS OR RE-ASSESS THE SITUATION CARE-FULLY
S → SLOWLY THEN
P → PROCEED/CHANGE YOUR PERCEPTION

This approach is illustrated by the old proverbs 'make haste slowly' or 'more haste, less speed'. Perhaps what we should say is 'more haste, more stress' or 'less haste, less stress'. Let's use the analogy of the car again. When you have to apply your psychological brake, imagine a set of traffic lights when you perceive yourself and your life going too fast. If you were actually driving a car, you know that the sight of the red light means stop. So you do this and wait until the light changes to amber. During the interlude while the light is red, you have time to assess and reconsider the next move. When the light turns to green, an incompetent driver (someone who easily gets flooded by stress) would accelerate rapidly, burn the car's tyres and ignore the possibility that another bad driver might jump the traffic lights or that a hurried pedestrian might be making a last minute dash across the road. This creates the potential for a disaster you want to avoid. You, being the safe and careful driver (someone who flows with events to minimise stress), slowly move on to the next priority, taking into account the other traffic and pedestrians on the road. Your perception of the situation and use of the technique embodied in the memory aid A WASP has helped you to avoid a disaster and to minimise your stress. This concept can be applied to all areas of your life which you perceive to be stressful and that threaten to flood you with resultant stress.

YOUR MISSION STATEMENT

Flowing with stress becomes easier if you formulate your own mission statement – a statement or a vision of goals that you would like to achieve. This also makes it easier to change your perceptions. Your aims can include short-term and long-term goals, and should be revised regularly as you progress along the path of learning to deal with your stress. Such a vision of the future is one of the most powerful predictors of success and happiness. It helps you to get a direction in life and to develop a clearer perception of what you have to offer the world, what to expect and how to cope. This makes it easier for you to flow. Research has shown that the consequences of not having direction can be widespread, resulting in a sense of disillusionment and lack of meaning. This makes it easier for you to be flooded by stress. Goals are crucial to encourage you to flow because they help you to formulate more clearly what you want out of life. If you are not sure, they also help you with self-analysis. A useful way to start is to simply sit down and make a list of the most important things you want to achieve. Revise this list weekly, as your goals are likely to change as their importance changes. A key point to remember is to be specific, not vague. For example, don't just write: 'I want to achieve specific things so that I have less stress.' Specify exactly in what areas and how you can achieve them. Narrow down your goals and be realistic – you can't have everything and there is little point in having goals that you think you should have but that in your heart of hearts are not really for you. Remember the five golden rules that help you achieve a goal: visualise it, say it, write it down (define it), share it, and do it.

CONCLUSION

In summary, different perceptions (Figure 8.1) produce different responses.

Two major reasons why not all people who are experiencing stress react in the same way and why some are not flooded by stress are rooted in: their perception of the stress and their ability to cope and to flow with events that could cause stress. This also explains why some people even find certain stress challenging. Individual differences play a role in identifying events that are stressful and in dealing with them. A person who is used to driving a car in a small rural town might find it overwhelming to drive in the rush hour traffic of a city for the first time. On the other hand, the city dweller who is familiar with the daily hassle of rush hour city traffic would be able to cope far better in driving through this traffic. In this example, individual differences stem from familiarity with the stressful event which allows a different perception and/or appraisal of it. This results in coping better with the stressful event. Your perception of how threatening the stress is and whether it will flood you or whether you will go with the flow is illustrated in Figure 8.3.

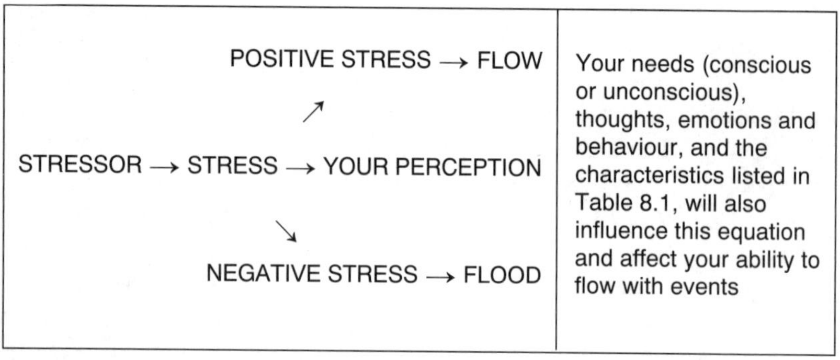

POSITIVE STRESS → FLOW ↗ STRESSOR → STRESS → YOUR PERCEPTION ↘ NEGATIVE STRESS → FLOOD	Your needs (conscious or unconscious), thoughts, emotions and behaviour, and the characteristics listed in Table 8.1, will also influence this equation and affect your ability to flow with events

FIGURE 8.3

There are several other key areas which I have found to be important if you want to prevent being flooded with stress. These other stress stoppers are discussed in the rest of this book. If you practise them, you can encourage a better flow in your life and reduce your stress. It all starts with the basic and initial steps of aiming for a perceptual shift and the characteristics of the flow response.

SUMMARY OF THE MAIN PRINCIPLES

- Harness your mind power to control your stress response.
- Use the energy of your emotions to work for you, not against you.
- Do this by learning to 'flow' with events rather than allowing yourself to be 'flooded' when confronted with stress.
- The ability to 'flow' is implicitly linked to your perception, flexibility and resultant thoughts, emotions and behaviour.
- Use your psychological brake to create time to reassess the situation before you proceed.
- Flowing with stress becomes easier if you formulate a mission statement.

CHAPTER 9

Be optimistic

OPTIMISTIC AND PESSIMISTIC ATTITUDES

OPTIMISM and pessimism are habits we learn as children. Usually our parents act as role models. The value of an optimistic and positive attitude in stress management can hardly be overstated. There is increasing evidence that a happy outlook can even positively affect disease. Around the world, optimists are life's greatest success stories. This is because they tend to have a challenging rather than a passive approach to life. Pessimistic people tend to look at stressful events that they can't control as internal – blaming themselves and feeling that it is all-embracing. Optimistic people tend to regard the same stress as external – feeling they could not have helped it, that it will improve and that the impact will not be that bad. Instead of being flooded by events, they flow with them. It is a habitual way of explaining setbacks to yourself. They attribute failure to temporary causes. Researchers call this an explanatory style that differentiates pessimists from optimists. Needless to say, optimists tend to cope better with stress. And there appears to be a distinct link between pessimism and not coping with stress. Pessimists usually believe bad events stem from permanent conditions. They allow one area of failure or disappointment to pervade their whole lives. Pessimists also tend to be unwell more often. One reason for this is that pessimism can produce more unhappiness and psychological problems such as anxiety and depression, as well as more stress which negatively affects the immune system.

BE PROBLEM-FOCUSED

Optimists tend to cope with stress by being problem-focused – that is, they focus more on what they can do about the problem that causes the stress, rather than how they feel about it, as discussed in Chapter 1. Such people have a higher expectation of succeeding (even if they do not do so immediately) because they do not just give up. This is the opposite of the emotion-focused coping often seen in pessimists. Pessimists usually think there is little they can do about their stress, and because they focus more on their negative emotions rather than on constructive action, tend to end up with poorer coping skills and more psychological problems. Optimists also tend to adopt an enthusiastic perception of life that leaves little room for negative thoughts and subsequent negative emotions and behaviour. This is in direct contrast to the negative spiral set in motion by the negative perception of life harboured by pessimists and their subsequent negative thoughts, emotions and behaviour.

Therefore, learn to be problem-focused in your stress-solving skills. By adopting a problem-focused, optimistic perception of life, you'll avoid negative thoughts, emotions and behaviour.

STAY IN CONTROL

People who feel they are in charge of their lives tend to have what psychologists call an internal locus of control. This means they have a general perception that their thoughts and actions are under their own control. When we feel we're the 'master of our own fate' we are better able to deal with stress.

The stress-inducing power of the perception of loss of control is equally important in all aspects of life, but particularly so in pessimists. Those with an external locus of control, feel their actions and what happens to them are beyond their control. Because of this, they often feel powerless and tend to respond less effectively to stress because they feel they lack the very sense of psychological empowerment required to cope better with stress. Locus of control can affect the mind and body in many different ways, but perception of not feeling in control of one's life, associated pessimism, negative thoughts and subsequent negative emotions can make it extremely difficult to cope with stress.

Pessimists have an external locus of control. They believe everything is beyond their control, out of their hands. This perception makes them feel powerless, and this snowballs into all aspects of their life but particularly stress control. If you feel you can't cope, you won't. The reasons for this are many: perception, associated pessimism, negative thoughts and emotions. So, stay in control.

HAPPINESS

The Chinese proverb 'with happiness comes intelligence to the heart' and sayings like 'a merry heart doeth good like medicine' and 'the joy of the heart makes the face fair' underscore the value of happiness. Optimists are happy people. For many, happiness is rooted in simplicity. Likewise, for many the modern tendency towards excess often impacts negatively on their psychological well-being and diminishes happiness.

LOCUS OF CONTROL

Locus of control describes the way in which people attribute responsibility for events that occur in their lives to factors within themselves and within their own control, or to factors outside of themselves and outside their control.

People with an internal locus of control believe they have an influence over the direction their lives take. They tend to be co-operative, self-reliant and knowledgeable about their work. They have a high sense of self-direction in their social and occupational lives, adapt well to change, associate with people with superior or equal abilities, believe in delegation, are achievement oriented and have lower anxiety levels. They also are generally trusting, self-confident, insightful, not dogmatic, and perceive authority figures as encouraging and supportive. They cope better with stress.

People with an external locus of control believe they have little or no control over the direction of their lives or the things that influence them. They tend to have unrealistic ambitions, not cope well with the demands of reality, have poor job satisfaction, be careless with equipment they are responsible for, rely on coerciveness and threats to get things done and cope badly with delegation. They also do not readily accept responsibility, blame others for outcomes they feel they have no control over and can be passive when they are faced with difficulties. Because they fail to exercise control over the environment, they do not experience the psychological success that makes them feel satisfied and gives them a sense of well-being. They don't cope well with stress.

There are many definitions of happiness and different roads to achieve it. But psychologists generally agree that we experience our greatest happiness when we focus on the frequency rather than the intensity of positive events in our lives. In this process, it is important to appreciate the little pleasures rather than always wait for a major single event, which puts us at risk of being disillusioned when the big event does not bring the happiness we anticipated. By our emphasis on waiting for the big moment of happiness, we allow ourselves to lose out on all the daily little things that can make us happy. Happiness also involves cultivating the perception that we ourselves contribute to the cause of these little events, and that we can prevent negative ones that make us unhappy.

ARE YOU SCARED OF HAPPINESS?

There are people who are scared of happiness. They often feel unworthy of it or they feel guilty when they are happy because others are so distressed around them. They might even erroneously believe that if they are happy, this will be followed by bad luck or misfortune. They often follow pursuits in life in order to disguise their unhappiness. For them (as for pessimists) the fear of losing is greater than the joy of winning. Psychologists have been stumped for years about what really makes people happy. Although there are still some uncertainties, there are also general agreements in this regard. It seems that what makes people happy today might be different from what made them happy long ago. For example, recent research has shown that people who watch TV soap operas could sometimes be happier than those who don't, because they seem to identify with the characters and plots and could even form imaginary friends with some of the characters. This does not apply to all TV watching though, as some programmes can be very distressing. Old keepsakes and souvenirs (even if they are of little monetary value) could sometimes bring more happiness than more expensive possessions. Likewise, money does not guarantee happiness. Satisfying relationships seem to be important for happiness as are certain personality characteristics found in optimists and extroverts. Sometimes work, sport or hobbies can make people happy, especially if they are challenged by these activities rather than stressed by them. 'Loners' and those who claim to be an 'island' without adequate social support networks tend to be less happy and have more difficulty in coping with stress. Research also shows that people who are happy and optimistic tend to fend off infections more than those who are not, because a positive frame of mind can help to boost the immune system. Happiness also helps one to stay young in body and mind, especially if one stays active because it makes people feel and act younger than they are. Happiness contributes to a good sex life, which in turn is one of the key factors on the 'long life checklist'. In as much as there are 'stress-seekers' (people who flourish on stress as discussed in Chapter 3), there are so-called 'sunny personalities' (people who are naturally pre-disposed to happiness). These people find it easier to relax and enjoy life's little pleasures. There is evidence to show that this could be partly genetically determined in some people. Happy people thrive, have better relationships, a more fulfilling life and tend to be more successful. They know how to re-charge their batteries and work on the assumption that things will improve, which is a self-fulfilling prophecy. They do not dwell on misfortune and know that a positive attitude is important. Happiness is about perception, thoughts and emotions rather than about what you have. In fact, some people can have everything in life and still be unhappy, because they pursue things that they mistakenly think will bring them happiness. Happy and optimistic people focus on the rewards of success, rather than on the penalties of failure. If you are aware of the barriers to happiness in your own life, you can make the necessary changes. So keep your sunnyside up – why spend your energy on worry or unhappiness when you can celebrate life!

Changing to the perception that there are many small positive events in our daily lives, contributes to positive thinking, positive emotions, acting happy, a sense of well-being and ultimately a better ability to flow with events and cope with stress. This is because life becomes more fulfilling and meaningful. Just like positive beliefs can produce wellness, so negative beliefs can produce ill-health. If you feed your mind with images of despair and negative thoughts, the mind eventually accepts them as the truth and the body responds accordingly.

SUPPORT SYSTEMS
Psychologists have studied perceptions, thought patterns and beliefs typical of many emotions from depression to euphoria, as these emotions relate to pessimism and optimism. Negative emotions differ from positive ones in the kinds of perceptions, thoughts and explanations that generate them. Consider, for example, loneliness. Loneliness is a personal and subjective experience of discomfort and psychological pain often related to the lack of intimate relationships. Loneliness consists of a cluster of emotions, including unhappiness, distress, a painful emptiness, feelings of isolation, apathy, feelings of drifting, futility, helplessness, oversensitivity, withdrawal and sometimes irritability or even suspicion. This can strengthen a perception of alienation from others, which can contribute to stress. There are two principal sources of loneliness: 'emotional loneliness', which can occur when people lack an intimate, stable attachment so they feel emotionally isolated; and 'social loneliness', which comes from a lack of friends and involvement in the community resulting in such people feeling socially isolated. If either form of loneliness lasts too long, such people may sink into a kind of pessimistic, self-critical state which leads to further deprecation.

SPIRITUALITY

Spirituality, religion and science are not necessarily at odds. A recent study showed that contrary to predictions many scientists still believe in God and religion. This study repeated a famous survey first conducted in 1916 by psychologist James Leuba, which predicted that disbelief in God would grow as education and knowledge increased. Contrary to the findings of the earlier study, new research has found that even if science and religion are often depicted as irreconcilable opposites, many scientists today continue to see no contradiction between a quest for knowledge through science and the belief in a higher deity and spiritual values. Spirituality and religion are not the same. Spirituality refers more to a frame of mind, whereas religion refers more to belief systems or worship. Both can involve powerful psychological states associated with healing and stress management. For example, prayer can assist in changing negative perceptions and beliefs into positive ones, and allow for the stress-reducing use of a single focus, such as relaxation, emotional catharsis, the mobilising of unknown energies and higher powers, and imagery and visualisation. In my own research on the theology–biology link and stress, I have found that religious discussions (volunteered by some patients) in group psychotherapy with cancer patients served both spiritual and communication needs for those who participated. My research supported the value of religious coping and/or 'spiritual coping' for some as a variant/dimension of psychological coping with stress. This research also confirmed the patients' belief that they have a right to expect respect for any spiritual aspects concerned with their treatment and their own experiences, and that a caring therapeutic relationship that respectfully incorporates such spiritual aspects contributes to a sense of emotional healing and the potential for inner healing. The research further showed that this helped them to cope better with the stress associated with their disease. Other research has shown that regular church-goers tend to have lower blood pressure than those who do not often go to church, and have reported the beneficial effects of cognitive-positive (as opposed to cognitive-negative) strategies such as praying and thinking about positive changes. The positive effects resulted in improved mood states, higher self-esteem, fewer concerns about one's condition and reduced levels of physical fatigue. However, although spirituality or religious affiliation and the sense of belonging to a fellowship for many seem to offer a buffer against stress and an additional pathway to healing, research has also shown that people who become obsessively involved can experience higher stress levels leading to distress. This was discussed in Chapter 3, when we considered brainwashing and stress. Nevertheless, throughout history the healing practices embodied in spirituality and religion have given rise to many accounts of remarkable recovery, discovering meaning to existence and stress reduction.

Many things can cause loneliness but important precipitators are age, disability, introversion, disease, isolation through loss of social activity or a loved one, low self-esteem, overdependence and shyness. Two additional sources that are especially relevant here are poor interpersonal skills and the inability to adapt to change, which further enhance the lonely, pessimistic person's perception of alienation from others. Loneliness, however, is not the same thing as solitude or being alone. Many people do things alone, live alone and do not feel lonely. Others have large circles of friends or live in big families and feel desperately lonely because they are not in touch with themselves or others around them. Often negative thoughts prevail in lonely people that no one understands them or cares about them. These thoughts are usually based on a negative perception of their interaction with their friends or family and make the loneliness worse. This sets in motion a whole negative cycle that frequently results in even poorer stress-coping skills. Take the example of the child who gets looks of non-love from parents and interprets this as rejection which then translates into feelings of not being recognised, or fear of abandonment and loneliness.

The value of spiritual nourishment, family, friendships and social support can be important factors in coping with stress because they can provide emotional support, guidance and a sense of belonging – something we all need. Not all support is affirming, though – the wrong support is occasionally offered, or you might feel claustrophobic from too much support or the timing of the support might be wrong. So it is important to recognise when support is adding to your stress or helping you cope better with it. That is, does it make you feel more optimistic or more pessimistic?

REACH OUT

Effective communication is an important tool to reduce stress. Many socially anxious people are poor communicators who then develop problems of loneliness. Their continued failure to maintain satisfying relationships can lead to a decrease in self-confidence and eventually an inability to initiate relationships in the first place, making the situation worse. In addition, when they do communicate, lonely and stressed people often disclose more negative than positive information about themselves. This makes other people uncomfortable about getting close to such a person. Everyone has problems and while it can be very supportive to discuss them with a friend at times, in general others don't always want to hear all the negative aspects of your life whenever they interact with you.

A key technique to deal with loneliness is to change your negative perceptions and to reach out to others by giving of yourself and your positive attributes and by creating opportunities for self-growth. You may find that your perception is often coloured by your need for acceptance, in which the overriding concern is dependence on others for your own sense of self-worth. In social situations, for example, you may routinely evaluate your own competence at performing socially and spend so much time wondering what is required to be accepted, that you miss the general flow of interaction. If this is your perception – change it to a more positive one. The other side of the coin is that you might want to reduce your stress in social situations by avoiding people, and in the long term you end up with a constricted social life rather than dealing with the stress and the feelings of loneliness. If this is you, reach out to others and strive for self-growth.

PUT MEANING INTO YOUR LIFE

Optimists move in a direction that makes life more meaningful. The Austrian existential psychotherapist and author, Victor Frankl, emphasises the uniqueness of humankind, our quest for values and meanings in our lives and our freedom to choose self-direction and self-fulfillment. He has offered many penetrating insights into the implications of the search for meaning. Your perception of stress can be usefully understood and approached from such an existential point of view. Change your perception from a meaningless existence to a meaningful one and take psychological charge of your existence. Don't fall into the trap of those who don't want to travel this road because they have the pessimistic perception that either they cannot do it, or that the outcome will automatically be negative or unrewarding. Stress management techniques can be of much more use if you are aware of your own strengths and you address the problem of meaning in your own life and your own philosophy of life. Accept personal responsibility for putting meaning into your life.

You'll find it useful if you combine an existential approach with the other recommendations in this book. This approach will help you to explore the very meaning of your existence and to face questions about your stress, life, meaning, existential isolation, loneliness, death and your free will. Your life is not exclusively determined by past experiences and you have some power over your destiny because of your ability to make choices, perceptual shifts and changes. You are who you are because you want to be. Because you are an interpreter of your stress, you can choose to make meaning of it since you are free to choose whatever interpretation you wish to place on the stressors in your life. This concept will help you cope and change your thoughts based on your perceptions of stressors and thinking errors. You cannot always change what is happening to you, but you can extract meaning out of your experiences and change how you see, think and feel about them – that is, how you allow the stress to affect you. If you do this, you emphasise your uniqueness as a person, your quest for values and meaning and your freedom to move towards self-direction and fulfilment. Putting meaning into your life will help you manage your stress better.

SEEING THE FUNNY SIDE

Healthy stress includes, amongst other things, an appropriate sense of humour. A daily dose of appropriate humour can go a long way towards becoming more optimistic and reducing stress. Humour has become an area of much psychological research. This is because it impacts on so many areas of our lives: it can positively reduce the fear of the 'fight-or-flight' response; it can help us get close to people through shared jokes and laughter; humour also reduces tension and conflict and places 'matters' in a different perspective; and it can diffuse stressful situations. Humour draws people closer to you. It forms an excellent buffer between pessimism, stress and negative perceptions. Research has shown that those who succeed in seeing humour or absurdity in negative news tend to show fewer negative emotions, are less prone to depression and cope better with stress caused by the anger or tension brought on by negative news.

Humour has strong cognitive elements, because it brings a new or alternative perception to a stressful situation and gives the person a chance to express emotions in a non-threatening way. This helps with regaining control. People who walk around with grim expressions all the time could experience difficulty in coping with stress. Humour can act as a buffer between the stress and negative perceptions that produce such a grim outlook. Seeing the funny side of something is a way of altering negative perceptions and through humour people can express their feelings indirectly.

THE POSITIVE EFFECTS OF LAUGHTER

Humour makes us laugh and laughter is good for stress management. Not only can laughter itself reduce tension and defuse negative moods, but it can also have positive physiological effects. The act of laughing stimulates the immune system and the release of endorphines in the brain which have known analgesic (painkilling) effects. Laughter also gives the person a brief physical work-out by increasing air-flow through the lungs and improving blood flow. When a person laughs it involves a simultaneous contraction of some 15 facial muscles! Some research has even reported that the sense of well-being gained from laughing 100 times a day is virtually equivalent to that achieved from rowing for 10 minutes.

People can use laughter in disturbing situations as a way to relieve tension and stress. Not all people laugh for the same reasons, but generally laughter and humour perform the basic functions of releasing excess energy and emotional tension. Researchers have noted that it is in fact possible to learn to be more humorous, especially if people take the time to find out what makes them laugh (humour is a very personal thing). Humour must be genuine, though, to be stress-reducing. This does not mean that you have to carry a smile all the time. Simply 'putting on a happy face', fabricating a smile or pretending to be happy (whilst masking psychological pain) will not be an effective stress-reducing technique. Likewise, laughing at the expense of others or humour that demeans others might create further tension and stress. Don't laugh at people – learn to laugh with them.

THE BENEFITS OF CRYING

To be optimistic does not mean that one should never feel sad or cry. Optimists, pessimists – everyone suffers loss and hurt. Appropriate weeping or crying can help relieve stress. Studies confirm that women cry more often and more intensely than men, and that most criers – irrespective of sex – feel better after crying. People who suppress crying (when they need to cry) deny themselves a potential stress outlet. Crying appears to be the opposite of laughter. Apart from the psychological purposes, it also has certain physiological ones. When crying, the person gasps for air in short repeated intakes or sobs and expels it through long sighs, which gives a degree of physical release. In addition, tears and the flow of mucous serves to rinse irritants from the eyes and nose. Incidentally, the tears produced from crying appear to be different from some other tears. Crying can also act as a release of tension, and especially of sorrow.

HUMOUR AND LAUGHTER

Humour is universal and laughter begins early in life. The average six-year-old laughs some 300 times a day as opposed to the average adult, who laughs only 17 times a day – which tends to confirm that some people develop a more negative perception of life as they grow older. A more disconcerting thought is that some research shows that as we enter the new millennium, people on average seem to be laughing less than they used to. People are 10 times more likely to suffer from serious stress-related problems such as depression now-adays than during the mid-1950s, when the average adult spent 18 minutes a day on laughing compared to the current average of only six minutes a day. When people are unable to live up to modern-day demands for success and progressive consumer exploits, they feel a sense of dissatisfaction, shame and failure. This is made worse when they compare themselves negatively with others whom they perceive to 'have made it' in life, resulting in further decline into a negative stress spiral. Laughter is sometimes connected with a release of aggression and hostility, which is useful for stress management. Also, through jokes we can express forbidden or unconscious ideas or act out anti-social tendencies in an acceptable, playful and funny way. Laughter and humour are, therefore, valuable social tools and stress reducers. They let people relax and become less inflexible and more receptive to new ideas, during which stressful, familiar and/or con-ventional situations and behaviour can be looked at from totally different angles. Incongruity often forms the basis of humour, be-cause in such situations we are prepared for one thing but quite another thing happens. Why this should make people laugh is not that easy to explain. We often know what makes people laugh, but why some do so more than others remains a matter for debate, as any comedian will tell you. What is more certain is that the element of surprise, without feelings of danger, can trigger off laughter.

The flip side of the coin is crying. Most babies cry briefly to take their first breath. It is difficult to say for sure whether these early cries reflect distress. However, they do serve other vital purposes such as clearing fluids from the respiratory tract and allowing the intake of gulps of air to inflate the baby's lungs. New-born babies do not produce tears for a while. When tears do appear, they keep the eyes moist and contain nutrients and various other components to protect the eyes from infection.

Crying can lead to excess tear production. When the natural drainage system of the eyes cannot cope with such extra tears, they overflow onto the face and down the cheeks. Tears can result from laughter, emotional distress, physical pain, yawning or other causes such as eye irritations. Research has shown that emotional tears contain different chemicals from those found in other types of tears, such as the ones produced when an onion is peeled. Two neurotransmitters reported in emotional tears are leucine-enkephalin, a natural opiate in the brain which is associated with pain relief, and prolactin, which is a chemical released by the pituitary gland because of stress (part of the endocrine system and the stress cascade discussed in Chapter 2). So it stands to reason that people can feel better from crying because through tears chemicals are removed that accumulate during stress. If you do not allow yourself the benefits of a good cry when necessary, you could be denying yourself appropriate stress relief because, like laughter and humour, crying can sometimes reduce stress.

Mourning can play a very important psychological role in dealing with emotional pain. We often hear expressions like 'a broken heart' or 'a lack of will to live' in people who have suffered bereavement. Today's science verifies centuries of belief that grief can cause sickness. Bereavement is psychologically very painful and extremely stressful. This emotionally harrowing experience can be eased through appropriate grief and mourning, thereby reducing the stress. So, trying to be optimistic does not always mean never crying – sometimes we need to mourn to 'let it all out'. Mourning can be distinguished from grief. It involves physiological and psychological processes and has a lot to do with the cultural customs and traditions of a particular society. Grief is a normal reaction of intense sorrow following loss, and such grief can be expressed through mourning. Grief is often the price we pay for loving.

CONCLUSION

Cultivating positive perceptions and thoughts involve a lot more than mere blind faith or simple acceptance of bad luck. To be optimistic, you have to learn to distinguish between things that you can and want to control and those you can't. As the saying goes: 'to change what you can, have the patience to accept what you can't and the wisdom to know the difference'. Tolerance and flexibility are essential if you want to learn to accept change, because they form the basis of positive adaptability. Intolerance and rigidity underpin poor adaptability because they contribute to pessimism, vulnerability and poor stress management. The important thing is to bounce back, put yourself back into psychological control and then remain in control. Remember, even if you can't change events, you can change how you feel about them. You can learn to emphasise the positive rather than the negative outcome of events by practising positive visualisation. Visualise a picture of yourself in your mind's eye as a calm, relaxed person who does not get phased by negative stress. If you have a positive picture of yourself for long enough, you will eventually always be drawn to it. We have seen how important a positive attitude and positive self-perceptions are. The one nurtures the other, while feeding into a positive psychological cycle that raises your stress threshold and keeps you in the positive phase of stress.

Stress is in the eye of the beholder because it is based on your perception of your stressors. It is really the way you look at the stressors in your life that will largely determine how they influence you and whether they will have a negative or positive effect. This in turn can also be influenced by whether you are an optimist or a pessimist. Optimists, in fact, see life events as challenges rather than stressors. They challenge negative perceptions and thoughts. If you are a pessimist, your perception will be distorted by your negativity and it will be difficult for you to make sense of what is happening. So think positively – you'll feel better and do better. Give yourself credit, set wise goals, change those pessimistic habits and rehearse being a winner. Optimism and happiness has a lot to do with broadening your views.

SUMMARY OF THE MAIN PRINCIPLES

- A positive and optimistic attitude is important for stress management.
- Optimists can flow with events, pessimists often get flooded by them.
- Optimists tend to be problem-focused when coping with stress, pessimists tend to be emotion-focused.
- Optimists tend to feel in control, pessimists don't.
- Optimists are happy people and less lonely than pessimists.
- Loneliness can make it more difficult to cope with stress.
- Lonely people often disclose more negative than positive information about themselves.
- Lonely people have more problems with interpersonal skills and adapting to change, which affects their social interaction.
- Like laughter, weeping can release tension.
- Healthy stress includes an appropriate sense of humour.

CHAPTER 10

Manage yourself

TIME MANAGEMENT

IN ESSENCE, effective self-management includes effective time management. If you can't manage your time, you can't manage your life, and poor self-management results in further poor time management. The end result is more stress. You don't want stress to manage you – you want to manage it. To gain control of time stress you have to be able to prioritise. The key is to plan, do and review. Remember, plans and good intentions are useless unless you follow them through with positive action. Inspiration is a start but unless it translates into action nothing will be achieved. Just making a list of the things you have to do is not enough.

Start by changing the perception that you are trapped in a time-cell that is not large enough for you. Being 'clock-driven' becomes a vicious cycle. When you have too much to do and too little time, you may end up doing everything half-heartedly. Not meeting your dead-lines will create even more stress, and so it goes on. The perception that there is not enough time is one of the main modern day stressors. Compensation claims for work-related stress problems resulting from time pressures and other work problems are increasing pheno-menally. Not only do many of these claims end up in court battles, but they are progressively related to requests for medical boarding on the grounds of stress. In my own work, I have found this to be one of the biggest demands made on my own time.

Time itself is not always the stressor, for time can also have a wonderful healing quality when we need 'time-out' to come to terms with certain stressful issues in our lives. More correctly, your percep-tion that you don't have enough time to do the things that you want to do, and use of time, adds to stress. Have you ever wondered why so many people struggle with time? A major reason is because they fool themselves about how much time they have available. They have a sort of fantasy about time, which is unrealistic. This feeds their misperceptions that there will always be enough time. Time is a valuable resource and it should be used as such, but not so that it causes unhealthy stress. It doesn't matter what you do, there are only 24 hours in a day. Neither you nor I can change that. While a change of perception in this regard will not put more hours in your day, it can help you to use the hours that you have more effectively, and thereby reduce your stress. A positive way to deal with this is by looking at effective time management techniques. Remember, time is a capital asset – something you cannot borrow, hoard or work harder to earn more of. Unlike money (which you can make more of to spend more), the only thing you can do with time is spend it. How you spend it will make the difference between success and failure, good and bad self-management, and coping or not coping with time-induced stress.

Now let's look at some other useful hints. Although most of these refer to time management at work, with a little adjustment and imagination many can be applied outside your formal work environment as well. You should spend your time wisely on all the important areas of your life that create a healthy balance in your lifestyle – that is, on work, relationships, social activities and even on animals and the environment. Time wasted in any of these areas is time lost. There are many reasons for poor time management. These include: poor organisational skills, the habit of working in a 'crisis mode', procrastination, not filling your day with quality achievements and poor management of your life which results in poor management and use of your time. Managing your life and your time better is your responsibility – don't blame others for not doing it.

Spend time on things that matter

Effective time management means spending more time on things that matter and produce results and less time on the things that don't. Cut out unnecessary work by defining your main goals and priorities and by checking in detail how you spend each hour in the average week. In doing this, you learn to manage your time, rather than spend it flippantly. You also have to learn not to do unnecessary things. Prioritise in terms of importance and urgency, in that order. List tasks you have to do first, second, third or not at all. Learn to spend more time on urgent matters and less time on those that are less important, and on those that you can't do, or don't have to do. Action you take can be divided into five broad categories:

- important and urgent (these are the tasks that must be done immediately or in the near future – they take precedence);
- important but not urgent (these are the tasks that divide effective individuals from ineffective ones – most of the really important things in life are not that urgent and can be done now or later, but because of this you never get around to them. Don't postpone them indefinitely);

- urgent but not important (these are the tasks that require immediate action, but are assigned a low priority);
- neither urgent nor important (often these can be diversionary and non-productive, but give you a feeling of activity and accomplishment because they keep you busy – it's a bit like spending the whole morning re-organising your office and files);
- wasted time (often to blame for your inefficiency).

Avoid overload

Evaluate the time needed for each task you have to do. Allow some time for the unexpected. Avoid overload, as the consequences of overload or overstimulation can lead to burnout. Time pressures, too much responsibility and the excessive expectations you place on yourself and on others, and similar expectations they have of you, are key contributors to burnout. The situation is exacerbated when, in addition, you lack work or social support and those around you also do not manage their time properly. Make sure that when you deal with people in terms of time issues and expectations, you don't fall into the trap of being in the same room but in different time zones.

Try doing the unpleasant tasks first. You will feel better afterwards and it leaves you with the pleasant tasks to look forward to. Don't do too much at once and learn to say no without feeling guilty. Be realistic – know your limits. Make the required perceptual shift. Avoid your work-load spiralling out of control, where you begin one task and in mid-stream you have to switch to another, and another and so on. Good self-management means setting deadlines and sticking to them, and being realistic in your time estimates. Be honest with your colleagues and your boss – tell them how you feel.

Delegate and update knowledge

If you look at your day-to-day tasks critically, you can eliminate many time wasters and learn to delegate more often. Remember though, you can only delegate effectively if you train your staff, or you will feel uncomfortable with the perception that they can't do it as well as you do and end up doing everything yourself anyway. People regularly need to go on in-service training or continuing education courses in order to update their knowledge and skills so that they are able to function better and more optimally in the work environment. Such continuing education is an essential part of modern life. Given the escalating knowledge explosion, it is said that on average knowledge dates every three years – that being the absolute maximum time you can afford the luxury of not updating knowledge. In some instances, such as in high-technology and other rapidly changing areas, there is a pressing need to stay abreast of development and change even more frequently than the usual three-year cycle update. For example, think of the socio-political transitions and changes in geographical boundaries in certain countries that have occurred in the recent past and continue to take place. So, you also need to regularly update your knowledge? Request assistance and further training if you feel you need this.

Free time

Protect your weekends and your free time. Avoid the 'Briefcase Syndrome' – always going home with a briefcase bulging with office work to do in your free time. Contrary to what you might think, successful people should carry slimmer briefcases with less unfinished work in them because they are better time managers. Those who are not, carry the large, bulging briefcases that lead to the 'Briefcase Syndrome', which is an indication that there is something wrong with their time management. Occasionally busy people might have to take work home or work in their free time. It's the price you pay for success. But you also need to get away from work, mentally and physically. In addition, if you constantly allow your work to spill over into your fun time, you are probably not practising effective time management and not living a balanced lifestyle. So take care of your private life and don't allow your home-life to become a stressor.

Bottlenecks

Bottlenecks (time binds that hinder the smooth flow of events) can occur for a variety of reasons, including failure to make decisions and prioritise actions. Because they waste time for everyone concerned, they are significant traps to avoid in appropriate time management. Start by looking for bottlenecks on your own desk and in your own behaviour, and sort out the clutter in your own life. Clutter makes for untidy thinking and planning, and hinders focused concentration on a specific task. It also leads to chaos and bottlenecks. Appropriate record keeping is vital, but excessive record keeping can be a symptom of insecurity and make the problem worse.

The old-fashioned 'efficiency consultant' has to a large extent been replaced by an 'effectiveness consultant'. Efficiency has to do with the best way of doing things, whereas effectiveness has to do with the best use of time, which may or may not be doing the things in the first place. Learn to manage by objectives. When you are trying to get things done and have a mental block, it can contribute to a bottleneck. You can deal with this by exploring a lack of facts or conviction you may have, or by looking for an appropriate starting point, and by remembering that fatigue interferes with creative thinking as does tunnel vision. Bear in mind the difference between striving for excellence and perfectionism. Perfectionism makes people vulnerable to depression because they make unreasonable demands on themselves so they are set to fail from the start. You can attain excellence, but perfectionism is virtually unattainable and the need for it will lead to stress and further procrastination.

Procrastination

'Procrastination is the thief of time.' It is on the side of wasting time and unfinished business, which in turn feed into bottlenecks. Until a task is completed, you haven't achieved your goal, and accumulating a backlog of half-finished tasks is a sure way to contribute to bottlenecks and stress. There is great wisdom in the sayings: 'Never put off 'till tomorrow what you can do today', 'No time like the present', and 'One of these days is none of these days'. If you are a procrastinator, do something about it. A good way to start is to use what has been called the 'Salami Technique'. A salami is not a particularly attractive-looking sausage that will stimulate your appetite. If, however, it is cut into thin slices, served individually, the original situation changes dramatically. Likewise, dividing a task into small, appetising and manageable steps that are immediately attainable will work wonders for procrastination. If it doesn't, write down the excuses you offer yourself not to get on with the task in hand, as well as the reasons why you should and benefits if you did. You'll be amazed at how quickly the benefits for you will outweigh the excuses. Do this in conjunction with the problem-solving techniques discussed in Chapter 13.

Travelling

As we saw in Chapter 6, commuting can be very stressful. If you have to travel to work, try to do this economically time-wise, and when at work try to eliminate further travel by making modern technology work for you, not against you. Consider, for example, using the telephone, modern fax facilities, e-mail or the use of a messenger service rather than wasting your own time going on errands. Self-management means knowing when to go to others, when to get people to come to you rather than you going to them and how to make your own and their travelling time cost-effective. The aim is to use travelling time effectively and productively rather than simply moving to and from work.

Interruptions

Interruptions are significant time-wasters. Although you cannot always eliminate them altogether, you can learn to minimise them by being more assertive and by improving your organisational skills. Using a secretary, assistant or colleague to keep unwanted visitors away at work can be a big help in this regard and a significant time-saver, because social callers and social chit-chat can be major time-wasters when work needs to be done. Learn to make appointments and see that you and your visitors keep to them. I find it useful to arrange for uninterrupted time blocks in the mornings where I can do everything that is important and urgent before I get on with the other business of the day. When meeting with someone and a degree of social chit-chat is unavoidable, try to keep this and other social pleasantries to a minimum. It's all very well to ask somebody how they enjoyed their leave or their weekend off, but it is not conducive to productivity and good time management if you allow the person to spend several hours explaining in-depth all the wonderful things they did during their time away. However, this does not imply that you have to be rude or offensive, which could add to further stress.

Try to keep telephone interruptions to a minimum. The telephone is a wonderful invention and a marvellous time-saver. But like anything else, it can be abused and end up being an irritating time-waster. Have a set time for receiving or returning specific telephone calls, when you'll be available and when it will be convenient for you to deal with telephone messages, etc. Be brisk and be decisive when using the telephone without being rude or unpleasant. In other words, cultivate a productive telephone technique.

Meetings

Don't call a meeting unless you have to. When I was a youngster, I always thought that going to a meeting somehow signified a degree of status – that I had arrived. As an adult I soon learnt that nothing could be further from the truth and that meetings can be both stressful and time-wasting if they are not necessary or appropriately conducted. If you do have a meeting, set a time limit and stick to it. Resign from committees if you cannot make a useful contribution, and if you do have to speak at committee meetings, make your points succinctly and briefly. Never go to a meeting unprepared. Don't try to do everything from memory. Make sure that you know your material, that your ideas are assembled in proper order and that you believe in what you say. It is very stressful to try to convince others of your ideas or products if you don't believe in them yourself. If the thought of this causes you stress beforehand, you could practise or rehearse your contribution before the meeting (even out loud if necessary) and visualise your participation. Taping or even video taping your performance and analysing it beforehand can assist you in this. An effective chairperson should:

- encourage new or shy members by asking for their opinion;
- control over-talkative members by summarising the points they make and then move onto the next topic;
- rule out misunderstandings by seeking clarification;
- make sure that you start and finish the meeting on time, make sure the objectives of the meeting have been met by bringing the discussion to a successful conclusion and considering whether the meeting was worth it;
- ensure that proper minutes are taken which should provide an accurate, balanced record of the proceedings. After the meeting make a list of what you did wrong, and one of what you did right. Keep this to help you with the next meeting.

Paperwork

Paper work can be a major time-waster. To prevent this:

- remove your name from the circulation list of junk mail;
- learn to skim read;
- don't write when a telephone call will do;
- be brief in your memos;
- use e-mail or a dictaphone (if used correctly, it can improve your productivity by up to 30 per cent);
- set aside time each day to deal with important and urgent correspondence;
- write succinctly, clearly and to the point;
- handle each piece of paper only once and avoid paper shuffling and reshuffling – many people waste time by correcting and recorrecting, writing and rewriting, or reading and rereading letters and memos;
- clear your pending tray daily and at the end of your working day clear your desk before you go home. It is very discouraging and stress provoking to come to work in the morning and find a huge pile of paper to deal with which you should really have dealt with the day before;
- use an appropriate filing system for useful material – useful enough to justify the time spent on keeping it;
- excessive record-keeping is a time-waster and can be a sign of insecurity. Keep the wastepaper basket close at hand – insufficient

use of it leads to excessive record-keeping, clutter and the perception of chaos;

- don't work or live in a clutter – it interferes with concentration on a single task and creates a feeling of being disorganised and 'stressed out'. Apart from the time-saving value inherent in keeping your pending tray, desk and filing tidy, it also encourages a tidy mind and reduces the perception that you work in a cluttered, stressful environment.

Keep a diary

A good diary can be invaluable to plan your time. It is a fairly personal item and there are numerous examples on the market to suit your particular needs. So, learn to plan your time better by keeping a diary, designing a work plan and keeping to it. Cultivate the habits of distinguishing between the things you have to do and those that can wait. Take personal responsibility for your time and for your priorities. Communicate these to others if necessary. Take regular short restorative breaks from work. These don't have to be rest periods, but simply switching for a few moments from what you are doing – make a cup of tea, take a short walk, or simply walk around the office, do a brief stretch or isometric exercise (tense and relax various muscles while you do deep-breathing exercises simultaneously), change from a sitting position to a standing one, etc. Short breaks provide relief from tension and monotony, refresh you and increase your effectiveness. Be warned, though, lunch breaks are necessary and useful. Use them as such – don't make them counterproductive by letting them run into two or three hours of wasted time. Using alcohol at lunch is a sure way to turn prime time into wasted time, poor concentration and afternoon lethargy. Review your work plan at the end of each day, week and month.

Relationships

Many people fail at work and in life because they persistently blame others for their own mistakes, poor communication skills and resultant poor interpersonal relationships. Look again at the list of defence mechanisms I discussed in Chapter 5. Are you using displacement or rationalisation by blaming others? Good communication and interpersonal skills are key issues in self-management, personal and work success.

If you have undesirable Type A characteristics (refer to Chapter 6), remember that they are not only stressful to you, but also to those around you. This doesn't mean that all Type A behaviour is problematic, but that you have to reduce or even neutralise the stress caused

by certain elements of this behaviour pattern. The particular characteristics that you have to modify are time urgency and lack of
planning ('hurry sickness'), simultaneous involvement in multiple
tasks (don't rush off to the next task before you have finished the first),
and your aggressive, hostile and sometimes defensive and possessive
behaviour. They often give rise to unnecessary misunderstandings
and stress in interpersonal functions.

A recent study found that aggressive, pushy men who monopolise
conversations, interrupt and compete for attention and who strive to be
socially dominant are 60 per cent more likely than others to die of
stress-related problems. This is because they are more chronically
stress-aroused and therefore release more damaging hormones. Although hostility is a tool used by dominant people to get their way,
dominant behaviour can sometimes be a method to control without
necessarily being hostile. This research found that dominant women
are less at risk of ill-health because to them dominance means something else. Unlike men who use dominance to get ahead for the sake of
getting ahead, women are more likely to use dominance as a means to
gather more support for their cause and for collaborating rather than
simply for competing. If you can reduce your ego-involvement, you will
go a long way in alleviating the stress your behaviour causes you and
others. An excellent way to achieve this is to change your perception
that you always have to be top dog, peerless and incomparable.
Tolerance, humility and modifying the stress-inducing aspects of your
behaviour will not diminish your performance and achievements but
actually enhance them in a far healthier way.

Remember that effective self-management is a basic ingredient of
happiness, and that it requires action, which in turn requires quality of
thought, alertness and sensitivity to your own needs as well as to
those with whom you interact. Don't waste your time with problem-
creating thinking. Develop a problem-solving mode of thinking, and
correct any thinking errors (see Chapters 13 and 14).

Management practice
Good management practice should take stress management into
account. Companies can do a lot to help. A first step is to recognise
that both the company and the individual have a responsibility for
employee welfare. It is important to get to know the needs of the
staff, to provide appropriate support systems, a satisfactory work
environment, acknowledgement for work well-done, training courses
and a good communication flow between management and staff. I
have found that many progressive companies offer stress manage-

ment courses which not only improve productivity, but leave staff feeling that the company cares. In fact, we know from research that a key element of good leadership is not domination but persuasion, which occurs when others adopt the goals of the group as their own on a basis of willingness. The idea is to build cohesive and goal-orientated teams because there is a direct link between leadership and team performance.

Lifestyle changes

Make the necessary lifestyle changes and watch your diet. Don't forget to set aside time for yourself. You need time to restore your equilibrium, to give your mind a 'space'in which to rest. There are many things you can do to achieve this outside your work environment – do something different, take regular holidays or go away for a weekend, practise relaxation, physical exercise, sport, etc. Many people find the answer in a non-competitive hobby or by doing something creative. In your quest for better management of stress, don't forget to stop and smell the roses or to appreciate the view along the way. Some of these activities will also help you balance your right-brain activity with that of your left brain, which is an important component of self-management and stress management.

LEFT- AND RIGHT-BRAIN ACTIVITY

Left-brain activity involves the systematic, logical part of the brain which controls movements on the right side of the body. Its cognitive style includes, amongst others: order and structure, processing information, rationality, logical and sequential thought, facts and figures, analysis and deduction, convergent thinking, dividing problems into bite size chunks and using well-defined plans, progressing with step-by-step precision, science and technology, good time management, and working things out carefully.

Right-brain activity on the other hand, involves the intuitive part of the brain, interpreting the whole rather than its parts, and controls the left side of the body. Its cognitive style includes, amongst other things: exploring the unknown and mysterious, opposites, abstract topics and artistic expression, body-image, crafts and creativity, ideas, feelings and emotions, the process rather than the outcome, perception, prayer and meditation, symbolism and fantasy, imagery, visual aids, graphic displays and dreams.

GOOD TIME MANAGEMENT MEANS YOU SHOULD . . .

✓ CHANGE THE PERCEPTION THAT YOU ARE TRAPPED IN A TIME-CELL.

✓ NOT BE CLOCK-DRIVEN.

✓ USE TIME AS A VALUABLE RESOURCE AND USE IT EFFECTIVELY TO REDUCE STRESS – IN ALL IMPORTANT AREAS OF YOUR LIFE.

✓ CHANGE THE REASONS FOR POOR TIME MANAGEMENT.

✓ STRIVE FOR BETTER SELF-MANAGEMENT AND ACCEPT PERSONAL RESPONSIBILITY FOR THIS.

✓ NOT PROCRASTINATE.

✓ SPEND MORE TIME ON THINGS THAT MATTER AND LESS ON THINGS THAT DON'T.

✓ DEFINE YOUR MAIN GOALS AND PRIORITIES.

✓ CHECK HOW YOU SPEND EACH HOUR IN YOUR AVERAGE WEEK.

✓ PRIORITISE AND COMMUNICATE YOUR PRIORITIES TO OTHERS IF NECESSARY.

✓ ALLOW TIME FOR THE UNEXPECTED.

✓ EVALUATE THE TIME NEEDED FOR EACH TASK.

✓ AVOID OVERLOAD.

✓ ELIMINATE TIME-WASTERS.

✓ DELEGATE MORE.

✓ UPDATE YOUR KNOWLEDGE REGULARLY.

✓ DO UNPLEASANT TASKS FIRST.

✓ NOT DO TOO MUCH AT ONCE.

✓ LEARN TO SAY NO WITHOUT FEELING GUILTY.

✓ SET DEADLINES, STICK TO THEM AND BE REALISTIC IN YOUR TIME ESTIMATES.

✓ PROTECT YOUR FREE TIME AND AVOID THE 'BRIEFCASE SYNDROME'.

✓ AVOID BOTTLENECKS.

✓ AVOID LIVING IN A CLUTTER.

✓ KEEP APPROPRIATE RECORDS AND FILING SYSTEMS.

✓ NOT WASTE TIME WITH EXCESSIVE RECORD-KEEPING, KEEP THE WASTEPAPER BASKET HANDY.

✓ MANAGE BY OBJECTIVES.

✓ DEAL WITH ANY MENTAL BLOCKS TIMEOUSLY.

✓ REALISE THAT EXCELLENCE IS ATTAINABLE, BUT STRIVING FOR PERFECTION WILL CAUSE STRESS.

✓ USE TRAVELLING TIME ECONOMICALLY.

✓ MAKE TECHNOLOGY WORK FOR YOU, NOT AGAINST YOU.

✓ AVOID INTERRUPTIONS THAT WASTE TIME.

✓ USE A DIARY EFFECTIVELY, DESIGN A WORK PLAN AND KEEP TO IT.

✓ USE UNINTERRUPTED TIME BLOCKS FOR IMPORTANT AND URGENT MATTERS.

✓ ENCOURAGE STAFF TO THINK FOR THEMSELVES.

✓ DEVELOP A PRODUCTIVE TELEPHONE TECHNIQUE.

✓ NOT CALL MEETINGS UNLESS YOU HAVE TO.

✓ STRUCTURE MEETINGS PROPERLY, SO THAT THEY DON'T WASTE TIME.

✓ RESIGN FROM COMMITTEES THAT YOU CANNOT CONTRIBUTE TO.

✓ ALWAYS BE PREPARED FOR MEETINGS.

- ✓ KEEP PROPER MINUTES.
- ✓ REMOVE YOUR NAME FROM LISTS OF JUNK MAIL.
- ✓ LEARN TO SKIM READ.
- ✓ BE BRIEF IN YOUR MEMOS AND WRITE CLEARLY.
- ✓ HANDLE EACH PIECE OF PAPER ONLY ONCE.
- ✓ CLEAR YOUR PENDING TRAY AND DESK BEFORE YOU GO HOME.
- ✓ REVIEW YOUR WORK PLAN REGULARLY.
- ✓ TAKE REGULAR, SHORT RESTORATION BREAKS FROM WORK AND DO NOT MAKE LUNCH BREAKS COUNTER-PRODUCTIVE.
- ✓ LEARN EFFECTIVE COMMUNICATION AND INTER-PERSONAL SKILLS.
- ✓ HAVE A MISSION STATEMENT IN WHICH YOU CONSIDER SHORT-TERM AND LONG-TERM GOALS.
- ✓ REWARD YOURSELF FOR EVERY SMALL SUCCESS – NOT ONLY FOR ACHIEVING BIG AND IMPORTANT GOALS.
- ✓ NOT SPEND YOUR TIME WITH PROBLEM-CREATING THINKING, BUT DEVELOP A PROBLEM-SOLVING MODE OF THINKING AND CORRECT YOUR THINKING ERRORS.
- ✓ MAKE THE NECESSARY LIFESTYLE CHANGES.
- ✓ SET TIME ASIDE FOR YOURSELF.
- ✓ BALANCE LEFT- AND RIGHT-BRAIN ACTIVITY AND DO SOMETHING CREATIVE.
- ✓ AIM FOR INCREASED PRODUCTIVITY WITH LESS STRESS AND MORE TIME FOR FUN AND RELAXATION.

CONCLUSION

Good time management equals good self-management. Such a person is motivated, interacts well and can handle pressures and stress. Never forget that better self-management leads to increased productivity, less stress, greater enthusiasm for your work and life and ultimately more time for fun and relaxation. Avoid the feeling of 'time poverty' (which means that you feel you never have enough time). Make time your servant and not your master so that you can live your life fully.

Look again at your mission statement and remember that for you to engage in good self-management and time management you also have to answer the following questions: 'What are my short-term goals?' and 'What are my long-term goals?' Don't punish yourself for failing to achieve these – rather reformulate and revise goals. They are not static and change all the time as you develop. Reward yourself for success and achievement of goals – even for small ones.

SUMMARY OF THE MAIN PRINCIPLES

- Effective self-management includes effective time management.
- Don't be clock-driven.
- Time itself is not always the stressor, it is your perception and use of time that cause stress.
- Spend your time wisely on all the important areas of your life.
- Accept personal responsibility for managing your life and your time – don't blame others.
- Learn effective time management skills, which are a basic ingredient for happiness and productivity.
- Protect your free time. Avoid the 'Briefcase Syndrome' – always taking work home.
- Balance left- and right-brain activity.
- Make the necessary lifestyle changes.
- Set time aside for fun and relaxation.

CHAPTER 11

Stand firm

ASSERTIVENESS

TO STAND firm includes being assertive and having a good self-image. Many people encounter stress because they have problems in these two areas. The essence of assertiveness is to balance your needs against the needs of others. This also has to do with the cultivation of good interpersonal communication and listening skills. It is necessary to be assertive when you want to practise good stress management. Assertiveness reduces conflict and stress. The first step in becoming assertive is to learn the difference between assertiveness, aggressiveness and submissiveness. These concepts represent three types of behavioural styles that people use when they interact with others. How do you perceive the difference?

Well, in a nutshell, aggressive people tend to deny the rights of other people in favour of their own. They often use demands or threats to achieve a win-or-lose result. This is a 'fight' response and the goal results in conflict. As opposed to this, submissive people tend to be non-assertive and deny their own rights in favour of those of others. This results in them being controlled by others, or excessive avoiding or accommodating behaviour. This is a 'flight' response and the goal is to ignore conflict. The accommodating component of this behaviour is aimed at 'harmony at all costs'. Characteristics of the submissive person include expressing thoughts and feelings indirectly, shuffling problems around instead of dealing with them and hoping that other people will be nicer. If you are such a person, what in fact happens is that people perceive what you say and do as something that can be disregarded because it is indirect. Both aggressive and submissive behavioural patterns are extreme and can cause stress or make existing stress worse, resulting in a 'flood' response.

As opposed to these two extremes, the assertive person's perception is: 'I have rights, you have rights. Since we recognise that, let's negotiate a win-win solution.' When you are assertive, you do not demand rights at the expense of the rights of others. Assertiveness does not mean deceiving or manipulating others. Assertiveness describes a kind of behaviour which helps you to communicate clearly and confidently your needs, wants and feelings towards other people, without abusing their human rights in any way. This is a 'flow'

159

response. Many stress-related problems arise because people are unable to express positive or negative feelings clearly. Assertiveness rests on self-respect and respect for others, but it also has the advantage of promoting such respect.

Obstacles to assertiveness include:

- a lack of awareness that you have the option to respond assertively;
- poor communication skills;
- anxiety about expressing yourself even when you know what you want to say is right;
- feeling constrained by conforming to stereotypes (lacking in originality or individuality);
- negative self-labelling (always thinking the worst of yourself);
- difficulty in making positive self-statements;
- difficulty in being direct and always choosing the indirect option;
- not being specific and using generalisations;
- a generally non-assertive, non-verbal behavioural manner that interferes with being assertive.

However, be careful not to overuse your assertiveness. You should make allowances for other people. Everyone makes mistakes, and by not allowing for the 'human element' in your interaction with others, you run the risk of engendering further tension and stress, rather than reducing it. You must look at assertiveness as a stress-reducing tool and be careful that it does not become stress producing. There is a fine line between being assertive and being aggressive. You have the right to protect both your physical and psychological space, but not by overwhelming others. At the end of the day you must like yourself and know that you have done what is best for you and that this was not at the expense of others. Recognise the difference between the positive and negative consequences of your assertiveness. Appropriate assertiveness also means being able to make responsible choices, exercising the need and/or right to protect your physical and psychological space and liking yourself in the process. There are effective and ineffective ways of doing so. Don't go overboard and cross the extreme boundaries by becoming either aggressive or submissive. Some of the many ways of increasing your assertiveness are listed further on. But it really all starts with first making that perceptual shift away from aggressiveness or submissiveness and then following these basic guidelines.

Then, accept that there might initially be a price to pay as you struggle to change and reorganise your old ways, and you begin to take control of your own life. In your quest to become assertive, try to decide exactly what you want. Next, decide if it is fair and ask clearly for it. Don't be afraid that you will risk other people's disapproval if you say no when you are uncomfortable with a request. To say no politely in such circumstances is one of the most effective ways of indicating assertive boundaries. Even if you run the risk of unpopularity, it is better to communicate to others that you don't need to sacrifice your values in order to be popular. Popularity is not the same as respect and being assertive means being respected and having respect for others and for yourself. Be calm and relaxed, communicate your feelings openly and honestly, give and take compliments easily and give and take fair criticism. Assertiveness actually leads to more fulfilling communication and relationships, because it reduces stress and releases positive energy towards others.

The assertive person is not driven by anxiety or excessive control, neither at work nor socially. In loving relationships, for example, assertiveness can result in a greater quality of intimacy because couples can express their needs, desires, fears, etc. honestly without fear of retaliation. Usually mutual need-satisfaction is of primary importance in loving relationships, and this can occur more healthily between mutually assertive partners.

Focus on appropriate verbal and non-verbal language (body language). Don't be submissive because you're frightened to deal with the problem and in the process allow others to take advantage of you. Although assertiveness leads to your living your own life without harming others, you can do this best if you don't beat about the bush, go behind people's backs, try to bully your way through interactions, call people names, bottle up your feelings or violate the dignity of others. Allow them to 'save face' if they need to change. You might even have to offer them options they hadn't thought about. Providing alternatives they can select from, can form both the basis of negotiating a 'win-win' solution and giving the other person some control in the process.

Assertiveness frees you from many stress-producing interactions, but remember that freedom embodies responsibility and not licentiousness or carelessness. Assertiveness means that you can accept responsibility for what happens to you in your life, but in doing so you can remain your own friend and retain your own dignity and self-respect. Because assertiveness can lead to defensiveness in others and perhaps make you defensive in return, it has the potential to trigger off a cycle that could result in aggression. Be prepared for this and act constructively by always focusing on the solution. Ask yourself these questions:

- Are you able to express positive feelings openly without harming others?
- Are you able to express negative feelings openly without harming others?
- Are you able to refuse requests without feeling guilty?
- Are you a good listener?
- Are you able to express personal opinions without harming others?
- Can you put action on hold while you give the other person a chance to air their feelings?
- Can you remain calm and dignified in the face of a hostile and angry outburst?
- Are you honestly able to compliment others without being insincere or using flattery? Flattery means insincere praise because you say things you don't really mean or that might not even be true. This does little to reduce stress meaningfully.
- Can you express appropriate anger without harming others?

DON'T BOTTLE UP YOUR ANGER

Bottling up anger is an inappropriate way to deal with stress. Expressing appropriate anger is not the same as losing your temper. Losing your temper implies that you are not achieving the psychological control that stress-management strives towards. No matter how bad things are, you can always make a situation worse by losing your temper. So learn to let your anger work for you, not against you. There are various constructive ways that you can use to manage your anger. Remember your psychological brake and applying the memory aid A WASP discussed in Chapter 8? You can also use it to control your anger. If you do decide to appropriately express your anger, think it through so that you achieve the results you would like. The ultimate aim is not only to make you feel good, but also to achieve the desired outcome. Try not to express your anger in the heat of the moment, but to delay it until your body's reaction has simmered down. Not only is it important to allow your body's state of arousal to get back to normal, but this period of self-imposed 'time-out' will also give you time to decide how to go about expressing your anger appropriately, and whether this anger is real or a symptom of something else like dislike or fatigue. To a large degree your anger depends on your perception of how the stress that triggered it off affects you, so a little bit of time will also give you the opportunity to re-appraise the situation and to see the problem from the other person's point of view. Rethinking the situation might make you realise that the trigger of your anger was not necessarily an intentional act of the other person.

SELF-IMAGE

Self-image depends largely on your perception of yourself and who you think you are. So, to improve your self-image, an initial step is to remember that you are what you think you are. This is true because you live up to the mental images you carry around with yourself. A negative self-image can be changed to a positive one, and a positive self-image is associated with positive attitudes and uplifting self-statements (or positive self-talk). Practice such uplifting and positive self-statements daily. Give yourself a daily pep talk. If you can learn to control your self-talk so that it is positive, it will make a great difference to your self-image. Programme yourself for success by constantly using positive self-talk. If you believe that you are unworthy and if you constantly engage in self-criticism, you will never improve your self-image. Learn to be kind to yourself and to be your own best friend.

If you find that you are shy and this affects your self-image, find your own comfort zone but break through feelings of being self-centred by focusing on the other person. Learning to give and receive compliments, cultivating the art of face-to-face talk, smiling and making eye contact, getting rid of thoughts of how silly you sound and look, and stopping yourself from assuming the worst will go a long way to help you. Don't forget, it is your perception of reality which affects you, and not reality itself. You have to change yourself first, before you can alter external factors. Your assertiveness, posture, the way you walk and talk, your level of mental and physical fitness and body language are all manifestations of your self-image.

DO YOUR EMOTIONAL HOUSE-CLEANING

Your self-image is also a product of past conditioning. You must accept that your future conditioning will also affect your self-image. So shed the emotional baggage of the past. Don't let it affect the present and the future. Do the necessary emotional 'house-cleaning'. This will also help you to improve your self-confidence and self-esteem. Your life is a bit like a ship with you in charge as the captain. You can steer it where you want to – into safe harbours, into storms or into smooth waters. Don't let your life's ship be weighed down by unnecessary and heavy cargo. If it interferes with your chartered course in life, cast it overboard. Make your ship lighter and easier to steer, with you in control rather than the unwanted baggage.

SELF-CONFIDENCE AND SELF-ESTEEM

Don't allow yourself to be someone who has become conditioned to lose, even though you were born to win. Self-confidence plays an important role in doing just that, so change that long-term perception of always feeling rejected and learn to be a little bit more group-centred. If you improve your self-esteem, your self-image and self-confidence will grow. So many people with low self-esteem often say that it has been present since childhood. This is probably true, because self-esteem has its early foundations in parental affirmation of the child's worth and in the child's mastery of early developmental tasks. When a child completes tasks successfully and receives adult approval as a result, that child should develop positive self-esteem. If you feel your early childhood was devoid of positive encouragement and positive affirmations from your parents or parent-figures, stop feeling like a victim and carrying such emotional baggage with you. Once you have changed your perception, and realise that you are not trapped in your past and can do something about it, you will think differently about yourself, and feel and behave differently. Positive self-esteem results from a feeling of being loved and the recognition that one is competent. Competent people feel 'they are able to', and 'they can'. Subsequently, a more positive self-esteem will be nourished in you by the development of new achievements and the values and standards of other important people in your life. Positive self-esteem is one of the most important keys to benefiting from opportunities in life. Try this simple exercise. Recall two of your previous successes and write down all the positive qualities you used at the time to achieve these successes. You still have them, so use them again now and regularly in the future, and add to them until you believe in your own strengths. You will soon learn that your self-esteem is the extent to which you believe yourself to be significant, capable and worthy. In short, you will learn to like yourself and be proud of who you are.

CONCLUSION

Remember, you have options other than the basic 'fight-or-flight' response, because of your thinking and verbal capacities. You don't have to be flooded by stress, because you can learn to go with the 'flow' of events. Being assertive will help you with this and with self-awareness, self-acceptance, honesty and openness, accepting other people as equals, aiming for win-win solutions, accepting responsibility for your own thoughts, emotions and behaviour and improving your self-image, self-confidence and self-esteem.

SUMMARY OF THE MAIN PRINCIPLES

- Standing firm includes being assertive and having a positive self-image.

- Assertiveness means being able to clearly communicate your needs and feelings towards others without abusing their rights.

- It is different from aggressiveness or submissiveness, which are extreme forms of behaviour that contribute to stress.

- A positive self-image depends on a positive perception of yourself, self-confidence and high self-esteem.

CHAPTER 12

Improve your communication skills

WHEN COMMUNICATION FAILS

OFTEN perception of communication, rather than actual communication behaviour, is at the root of a problem. This is well illustrated by an easy technique for measuring how communication fails and how to correct it, developed some years ago for use with couples and called 'Zapping'. A 'Zap' is when you hurt the other person by what you say, whether you intend to or not. If the other person perceives it as hurtful, it is a 'Zap'. The idea is to count the number of 'Zaps' exchanged between two people in a day. By quantifying them, the couple can then work towards reducing them. A key issue is, when someone perceives a communication as a 'Zap', the 'Zapper' can't simply wave it aside by saying, 'I didn't mean it.' Whether the person who caused the hurt intended to or not, the other party still experienced it as hurt and, therefore, communication was ineffective.

'Zapping' can also be used to improve communication in other situations. To improve communication and reduce the number of 'Zaps', always start with something positive when you state the problem and be specific. Admit to your role in causing stress and discuss one problem at a time. Avoid being negative, try to stay neutral and focus on solutions. Avoid mind-reading and be specific about any changes that you agree on.

Communication breakdown is often a contributing factor to loneliness, whether it occurs at home, socially or at work. Incidentally, the question of what makes loving relationships work is frequently put to me by patients. In my experience they work when they are built on values – genuine values – and mutual satisfaction of needs. These issues must be shared because closeness cannot occur or thrive without honesty and assertiveness. There should also be mutual support and praise and sharing of responsibilities. No relationship can be perfect all the time, but love will not survive with constant criticism. Loving relationships also work when those involved share their emotions and work together through the hard times, give and forgive and work towards a self-definition (that is, who you are, what

166

you want and how you are going to achieve it). Furthermore, self-love and self-definition helps those involved to relate to each other and to others. Once you have found love, treasure and maintain it – it won't run on its own energy if you do not provide the fuel to keep it going.

OBSTACLES TO GOOD COMMUNICATION
In general, methods of communication constitute words, tones, visuals and body language. There are several impediments to hamper good communication. Let's use the example of the car again. If you want to drive smoothly and safely, you have to watch out for hazardous barriers. Some are overtly dangerous (like warnings that alert you to major road obstructions), while others are more subtle (like overtaking or changing lanes). Likewise, there are some common barriers to good communication. Some of the most important ones are mentioned here.

JUDGING OTHERS
The well-known American psychologist, Carl Rogers, believed that a major obstacle to good interpersonal communication is the tendency to judge others. He believed that effective therapists should be genuine and honest when listening to others expressing their feelings. They must seek accurate and empathic understanding of the problems presented to them and they must display a warm, unshakable, non-judgmental regard for the other person. I believe this applies equally well to all forms of good interpersonal communication.

LABELLING
Variants of judging people involve indulging in criticising or name-calling. A good example of this is the poor communicator who plays amateur psychologist by expressing an uncalled for, usually incorrect diagnosis, such as 'you're an idiot.' This is really a comment on the person's level of intelligence, although it may not always be perceived as such. Sometimes the poor communicator labels people, such as 'you are always lazy,' or 'you can never get anything right.' Such communication styles only serve to demean the person being critised. If this happens to people, they will feel discouraged and be afraid to aim higher, because they've been conditioned by negative remarks to assume that they will fail. Such self-doubt obviously leads to a poor self-concept. And the labelled person begins to live up to other's negative expectations – a self-perpetuating cycle.

Labelling-theory has been a long-standing research area for psychologists who are concerned that, once a label is attached or attributed to a person, it becomes too easy to accept that label as a type of description of the person without further inquiry. It never fully describes the person but just some aspect of a perception of that person's behaviour or current functioning. This results in preconceptions and misconceptions about the person, which make it difficult to be objective about him or her, leading to inaccurate pre-expectations which in turn negatively affect interpersonal communication. Another problem is that such preconceptions or misconceptions are communicated to the person, who may accept this 'false' identity and behave according to the expected role, and develop a likewise perception that can be very harmful and highly stress-inducing, in which morale and self-esteem can be further devastated. This self-fulfilling prophesy has been referred to as the 'Pygmalion Effect'.

SEND OUT THE CORRECT MESSAGE

The opposite style of communication to negative labelling is also destructive. Good communication demands honesty. Praising someone when both of you know it is undue praise, is damaging and manipulative. Effective communication requires that a true and correct message is conveyed and received. Sending out a wrong or false message is sure to act as a communication barrier, as can ordering people around, threatening them, demoralising them, questioning them excessively and giving inappropriate advice.

At the same time, avoiding the concerns of others (the tendency to divert from the other party's message) does not facilitate good communication. For example, someone comes to you and talks to you about their problem, but you are so busy trying to tell that person about your own problems that you don't listen to them. You simply avoid the other person's concerns by focusing on your own or you use a defence mechanism like rationalisation or denial. Alternatively, you may enter into arguments about it, or try to reassure the person inappropriately (or sometimes falsely) by saying: 'Never mind, everything will come right,' without really tackling the issues at hand. This just destroys trust between people. Other related communication barriers include misinterpretation, hidden agendas, preconceived ideas and a lack of self-awareness.

We have seen that stress can be one of the biggest contributors to depression. There is a direct link between stress caused by interpersonal problems and depression. If you have poor interpersonal skills, you face a higher risk than others of experiencing psychological problems. This is because not being able to relate to others can cause stress and this, in turn, may produce other problems. By learning to resolve conflict between you and others, you avoid this downward spiral. This is, in fact, exactly what many therapists focus on with depressed patients – teaching them to resolve interpersonal problems through improved communication.

COMMUNICATION STYLE

How can you improve your communication skills and thereby reduce stress levels? When you were born, your communication skills were extremely limited, designed to focus on your primary needs of comfort, hunger, thirst, etc. (as illustrated in Figure 7.14). Your subsequent style of communication is essentially something you learned in one way or another from parents, teachers, friends, the media, actors you admired in the movies, etc. If you were taught poor communication skills, you can unlearn them and replace them with more desirable and effective communication skills and ways of relating to people. All it takes is practice. You can start by avoiding the barriers discussed above and by cultivating good interpersonal skills, as well as a pleasing personality. There are certain basic desirable characteristics in a pleasing personality. How many of you could sit down and make a list of the most desirable ones that can promote good interpersonal and stress management skills? It might be an interesting exercise if you jot down some of the qualities or characteristics that you think you should cultivate to do that, before you read on. Table 12.1 lists, in no specific order, some of the most desirable characteristics that facilitate good interpersonal communication and effective stress management.

BODY LANGUAGE

Communication is not restricted to verbal exchange – non-verbal communication (body language) is equally important. Effective communication hinges on providing feedback, creating an atmosphere helpful to communication and clarity about why and what we want to communicate. It leaves people feeling good about themselves and as such forms a basis for change. But it also involves non-verbal communication, such as appropriate eye contact, tone, gestures, posture, etc. We can communicate our stress to others sometimes without saying a word.

Body language forms an important part of stress management, and is perhaps the most common form of human communication. Undue stress is readily reflected in non-verbal communication. Consider, for example, the role of facial expressions as non-verbal communication. They reveal many combinations of emotions and stress. Facial expressions are probably one of the most readily observed gestures, since we tend to focus more often on people's faces than other parts of their bodies. A frown may reflect displeasure or confusion; a raised eyebrow, envy or disbelief; a squint and tightening of the jaw muscles, antagonism; and a sideways glance, interest or coyness.

TABLE 12.1

DESIRABLE CHARACTERISTICS THAT CAN PROMOTE GOOD INTERPERSONAL AND STRESS MANAGEMENT SKILLS
✓ SELF-AWARENESS ✓ SELF-CONFIDENCE ✓ EMPATHY (NOT SYMPATHY) ✓ POLITENESS ✓ RECEPTIVENESS TO NEW IDEAS ✓ FLEXIBILITY AND THE ABILITY TO FLOW WITH EVENTS ✓ A POSITIVE ATTITUDE ✓ SINCERITY ✓ HONESTY ✓ GOOD COMMUNICATION SKILLS ✓ GOOD LISTENING SKILLS ✓ GOOD SPEAKING SKILLS ✓ GOOD CONFLICT RESOLUTION SKILLS ✓ A SENSE OF HUMOUR ✓ ASSERTIVENESS ✓ PATIENCE

Emotions or stress are commonly reflected in people's eyes. Even pupils of the eyes open and close as a result of emotional reaction, and it has been shown that the greater the interest the person has in a particular picture, for example, the more the pupil will dilate.

How often have you heard expressions such as: 'That person has shifty eyes, or beady eyes, or snake eyes'; 'Her eyes are inviting'; 'We don't see eye-to-eye'; 'She gave him the evil eye'; 'That is a hateful stare'; 'That is a forceful gaze'; 'A look that could kill', and so on. These can range from one extreme to another, from an aggressive and hostile gaze, to a 'poker face', to a 'blank look', to a 'choir-boy look' with half-closed droopy eyelids that may or may not reveal true intent.

Be aware of possible differences in this regard. Researchers in body language have noted that in some cultures people make eye contact more often when they listen than when they talk, and that

NON-VERBAL COMMUNICATION

It is difficult for people not to communicate because, even if they do not talk, they still behave (non-verbal communication). If you are with somebody you love, in a warm and accepting environment, you often don't have to speak a word – your affection will be understood. Interpreting (reading) body language (or non-verbal communication) is one of the most important skills for effective communication, because a relatively small part of communication is gained from verbal expression. After all, before verbal language developed, body language was one of the most important purveyors of communication. Some authorities have found that about 35–45 per cent of communication is verbally derived (10–15 per cent words and 40 per cent tone) and the rest comes from body language and visuals, whereas others say that the overall verbal impact when you communicate is about 7 per cent verbal as opposed to a 93 per cent non-verbal. The gestures, postures, facial expressions and looks that make up body language can reveal a lot about people, although the messages they convey are not always that clear. There are cultural variations and sometimes body language gives messages that might not be intended. For example, a bank manager might look stern even if he or she feels sorry for the customer who wants to borrow money, or a shop assistant might smile at a rude customer even if he or she wants to rebuke them. So remember the old Chinese proverb: 'Watch out for the person whose stomach doesn't move when he or she laughs.' On the other hand, body language can reveal true thoughts and feelings. For example, the person who sits rigidly with arms and legs crossed could be seen as aggressive or aloof, whereas the person who slouches or shuffles along with their head pulled up between their shoulders and not noticing anyone around them, could be dejected or depressed. There are also differences between the sexes. For example, men tend to point their fingers and women to nod their heads when indicating something. If you can read the signals of non-verbal communication you can get a good idea of the person's stress levels. Look out for the behavioural reactions described in The Stress Symptom Checklist in Chapter 5, p. 44.

there are cultural exceptions in the amount of eye contact that people make. Furthermore, a key to body language in society is often propagated by social norms and rules of etiquette, so that body language is partly influenced by culture. However, there are certain universal expressions of body language, such as in facial expressions like anger, happiness, fear and sadness, which are common to all cultures.

The face we present to the outer world is not always our real face, and just as we use psychological defence mechanisms as psychological masks, so we use facial masks to hide our true feelings. A person may accidently cut you off with their car in a parking garage, but their smile says: 'Please forgive me, that was a silly mistake.' Your reaction, in turn, might be different and you might scowl. Incidentally, apart from what I have already said about the psychological symbolism associated with cars, one reason why some drivers tend to be so affected by driving behaviour is that a car creates the perception that their body zones have been extended, giving them a false sense of psychological expansiveness.

Some people smile their way through the day but may hide a host of other emotions beneath this mask. However, this masking process can go beyond facial expressions and involve the entire body. A woman may sit in a certain way with legs crossed to conceal her sexuality, and a man may assume a certain posture to state his ownership of something. He might, for example, lean on his car in a very possessive way while having a conversation, and through body posture announce to the observer that this is his car. Certain men are very threatened when other men approach their girlfriends. They stake their claim by putting their arm around the girlfriend's waist.

Sometimes people drop their masks to reveal their real selves. Even if a person stops communicating verbally, the same person's body language continues to communicate through countless other non-verbal signals or even the absence of body movement. An extreme example of this is seen in severely disturbed people who ignore the inhibitions imposed by society, and disregard the most commonly accepted masks, for example by neglecting personal hygiene or clothing and becoming involved in confused verbal and interpersonal communications.

LISTENING SKILLS

A good communication technique is to display interest in others by asking them questions about their prime concerns. In order to do this we need to be effective listeners and cultivate good interpersonal, speaking and conflict resolution skills. People who have difficulty in dealing with stress normally don't listen well. More often than not they pretend to. Listening is more than hearing – you can hear what is being said, but that doesn't mean that you are listening effectively.

The art of listening is the key to good interpersonal communication and a prerequisite for influencing others. It includes discovering and 'reading between the lines' of what is being said. Good listening makes for more emotionally mature, more democratic and less defensive and authoritarian interaction. This can also enhance self-esteem, because it reduces the stress associated with feeling that your ideas are not being taken seriously.

You should acquire good listening habits if you want to be a good communicator and if you want to manage stress. There are numerous ways to do this. A first step is to consider what poor or good listeners do.

POOR LISTENERS TEND TO . . .

- not listen when they have no interest in the particular subject being discussed.
- not pay attention, or fake attention.
- display emotional or behavioural reactions (whether positive or negative) that can upstage the degree to which they listen – for example, positive reactions might be demonstrating excessive enthusiasm and negative ones are shown by getting agitated.
- not listen for facts.
- interrupt the speaker in mid-sentence.
- feel defensive.
- listen for things to disagree with.
- use platitudes and clichés.
- give false reassurances.
- pass judgements.
- lose their objectivity.
- not check that they understand.
- demean the problem.
- expect to be attacked.
- be passive listeners.
- listen only to the words being spoken and not hear the meaning.
- hide behind words.
- ignore body language and feelings.
- be intolerant of distractions.
- create distractions.
- devise a reply before the speaker is finished.
- listen only for what they hope or want to hear.

GOOD LISTENERS TEND TO . . .

- establish good rapport between themselves and the speaker.
- understand the speaker's frame of reference.
- listen for what is not being said.
- listen for patterns – they have an ear for the finer themes being expressed.
- listen for discord.
- have empathy (not sympathy) – understand people rather than feel sorry for them.
- recognise their own prejudices and not allow them to interfere. For example, one of the more common prejudices in society these days is ageism, a prejudice against the aged – such a prejudice would interfere with effective listening if an old person is speaking.
- cultivate the habit of asking questions and verifying the facts.
- continue to concentrate, even if they do not agree with the speaker or even if the speaker's message becomes difficult or boring.
- be patient.
- keep their temper.
- be alert.
- avoid putting undue emphasis on single words or phrases in a message, but wait for the completed message before responding.
- demonstrate respect for the other person's viewpoint.
- concentrate on the speaker's message.
- not base their conclusions on isolated facts.
- avoid premature evaluation – they listen to the whole story before they form an opinion.
- demonstrate interest.
- minimise distractions and interruptions.
- resolve conflicts or potential conflicts.
- not be too passive or overactive when they listen.
- try to strike a balance between their and the speaker's verbal exchange.
- seek clarification of what the speaker is saying.
- summarise key points by, for example, saying to the speaker: 'Is this what you mean?'

Effective listening is an art as much as a skill. The perception that being a good listener simply means sitting back in your chair and saying nothing is a misperception. Listening is a complex process which involves an active rather than a passive response. You don't have to agree with the speaker to be an effective listener, and in fact disagreement can often result in a more useful interchange of ideas because it makes you concentrate on what the other person is saying. Finally, good listening skills go hand in hand with appropriately noting and interpreting body language and non-verbal communication.

SPEAKING SKILLS

Good communication also means the ability to speak well and to communicate your thoughts appropriately. How do you learn to do that? In order to cultivate good verbal skills you can start by avoiding the use of words such as 'sort of', 'I should have', 'I would have', which indicate a lack of confidence. Don't ramble and repeat at great length, and don't trail off without finishing your sentences. Some people tend to start a sentence clearly, but then end up muttering towards the end, so that often the listener cannot really hear the end of the idea expressed. A useful technique is to find a good role model. Study that person's way of speaking. Another useful technique is to analyse your own voice. You can do that easily by listening to a tape recording of yourself speaking, and establishing whether you:

- use language that makes you appear weak and unsure.
- are tentative in what you say.
- talk in a sing-song way.
- are too questioning.
- speak in a nasal, whiny, negative or unhappy child-like tone so that no one can understand you.
- sound apathetic, monotonous, aloof.
- have any irritating speech tics like 'mmm' and 'ah' that interfere with the flow of your speech.
- trail off without finishing sentences.
- speak in such a way that it puts you at a disadvantage.
- speak too slowly or too rapidly – a rule of thumb is that about 170 words per minute is considered to be a good speaking rate, so measure your speaking rate and try and work on improving the pace of your speech.

You will feel less stressed if you understand those you speak to, and feel you are being understood by them.

YOU CAN IMPROVE YOUR MANNER OF SPEAKING IF YOU . . .

- project your voice.
- use inflection and modulation – vary your tone of speech.
- identify and correct problematic speech habits.
- pace your own speaking.
- learn how to present yourself suitably.
- speak to a mirror to gauge the visual effect.
- enunciate clearly.
- use appropriate body language/eye contact.
- learn to become a persuasive speaker with self-confidence.
- make sure that you are always prepared when you have to speak in public or at meetings.
- enrol in a course where you can learn to become an effective public speaker, if you continue to find it difficult to do public speaking.

CONFLICT RESOLUTION

Some people develop a fear of being assertive because they dread retaliation. You might end up not really making the point you want to make, and thereby the conflict is often not resolved. Don't be afraid of assertion. Don't fear rejection or confrontation because you don't want to relinquish your own rights, as long as they are fair and just. Remember, you have a right to appropriately defend your beliefs. Don't teach others to take advantage of you by relinquishing them. Express your feelings honestly, openly, directly and appropriately. Tell others how their behaviour affects you, especially if their behaviour affects you negatively. In this process, though, you should respect the rights of others and give them the opportunity to change their own behaviour. Remember, negotiating should ideally always result in a win-win solution. Never negotiate the other person into a corner. Give them an honourable way out, and when you feel downtrodden or mistreated, rectify the situation. Don't walk around with suppressed anger or frustration. If you can ensure that others acknowledge your needs, you'll gain not only their respect, but also your own self-respect. Learn to say no without feeling guilty.

When you consider these pointers to help you to reduce conflict, remember that there is a direct relationship between stress and conflict. Conflict leads to frustration which in turn may exacerbate stress, thus making demands on your coping skills. We saw earlier that defence mechanisms can serve various functions. They can be used to keep emotions within bearable limits to reduce stress, restore psychological balance and provide 'time-out' to help with the adaptation needed to deal with stress and unresolved conflict. When psychological defence mechanisms fail to deal with the frustration associated with conflict, our stress gets worse because of resultant inadequate conflict resolution. We experience frustration when we encounter obstacles along the way, when our goals or activities are blocked. We then respond to such frustration emotionally by getting angry, despondent, aggressive, etc. and becoming stressed.

An effective method to combat frustration that prevents you from attaining your goals, is to make a perceptual shift towards more suitable alternatives. A useful way to do this is to try to answer the questions: 'Why do I really want to do this?' and 'What are my expectations if I do it?' This will help you to look at your goals from a different perspective. Frustration uses energy which can be better spent on resolving the associated conflict, so look for alternatives that can be readily implemented to decrease your stress levels. Typical types of conflict are:

- a barrier between you and the goal because your goal is thwarted, resulting in conflict;
- approach–approach conflicts (conflicts arise when you have to choose between two positive goals);
- avoidance–avoidance conflicts (conflict arises when you have to choose between two negative goals);
- approach–avoidance conflicts (conflict arises when you are both repelled and attracted by the same goal); and
- multiple approach–avoidance conflicts (conflict arises when you have to choose between several positive and negative goals).

The strength of positive and negative goals is affected by their psychological distance from the person who has to make the choice – that is, the closer you are to a positive goal, the more it attracts you, or the closer you are to a negative goal, the more it repels you.

CONCLUSION

Studies have shown a consistent link between communication problems and stress at all levels of interaction, but especially in close relationships. A paradox of our times is that while electronic and media communication have made strident leaps, the same cannot be said for one-to-one interpersonal communication between humans. Electronic bridging of the communication gap has been nothing short of amazing. The internet, opening up a whole new world of communication at the touch of a few buttons, is a case in point. However, while all this is happening, people are not doing well interpersonally in their communication, especially regarding stress management. People in non-stress relationships pause to acknowledge that they have understood each other's difficulties. Communication deficits are most often manifest when there is lack of such understanding and a conflict of interest.

SUMMARY OF THE MAIN PRINCIPLES

- Effective communication is essential for stress management.
- Avoid communication barriers.
- Cultivate good interpersonal skills, effective listening skills, effective speaking skills, effective conflict resolution skills.

CHAPTER 13

Develop a problem-solving mode of thinking

YOU ARE A THINKING PERSON

A N ESSENTIAL part of dealing with stress is the ability to solve problems effectively. The way you initially perceive the problem (stressor) could result in a feeling of being overwhelmed or flooded by the resultant stress – the 'flood' response. Your thinking patterns are important in stress management because, for example, your knowledge affects how you perceive stress. An important skill is to learn how to use thinking to solve problems to reduce stress. People who succumb to the 'flood' response have often learnt to do the opposite – they use their thinking to create problems and cause more stress.

Many of the life events and stressors that you are exposed to can be construed as problems to be solved. To solve a problem, you have to represent it clearly in your thinking processes. You have to become consciously aware of yourself as a thinking person who can solve problems. Take, for example, the stress of a driving test: it may be so overwhelming that you feel your mind goes blank so that you don't know what to do next. Realise that what actually happens is that your mind is filled with all sorts of outside thoughts and feelings that prevent you from focusing on your current performance. You should remind yourself that you are a thinking person with the capacity to solve the problem.

PROBLEM-SOLVING SKILLS

The following method is a useful way to solve problems. Firstly, define the problem accurately. The way you initially present the problem to yourself is critical to working out a solution. In defining it accurately, you have already started to solve it. Often what you perceive to be the stressor you are confronted with might not be the real problem that is causing the stress. A practical example is illustrated by a stressed out patient who comes into the casualty area of a hospital with a fractured femur following a motor vehicle accident. The casualty doctor is called to see the patient. The question now is: 'Which problem is causing the patient's stress?' 'Is it the fractured femur?' 'Is it the

179

accident?' The nurse says: 'Doctor, the patient is intoxicated.' Question number three: 'Is the real stressor the patient's drinking problem?' When the social worker comes to discuss the problem, she says: 'But I know this patient. He doesn't normally abuse alcohol. His wife left him yesterday.' Now, is that the real problem? You see, you need to define the problem precisely if you want to deal with the stress it causes. Once you have defined it accurately, you divide the problem into manageable units to avoid the perception of being flooded by the stress of the overall problem. Think in microsteps. Once you've broken the problem into smaller units which you can manage individually, the sense of being overwhelmed by the overall stressor (the original bigger problem) is likely to disappear. Try to keep the smaller units few and simple. Complicated ones and too many choices are a recipe for disaster and can result in conflict and further stress. Then tackle each of the smaller units individually by applying heuristics (the art of discovery and taking thinking short cuts). This also involves a real desire to find out more, exploring assumptions based on your past experiences, your gut-feeling, your background and your training and knowledge. These short cuts often prove effective. For example, if you parked your car in a busy parking garage at a shopping mall and want to find it quickly, you might first look for the colour or some other point of recognition. It is only when you get to the car that you make sure that it is really yours. As you work with the smaller steps and the situation becomes clearer, you can put them together and eventually switch to the larger picture (macrostep).

However, sometimes thinking short cuts does not work that well and you will need a further key ability to successfully find solutions. The answer is a technique called productive thinking. This technique also involves using your previous experience and knowledge, or even that of others. Some people augment their own thinking ability by the creative use of computer programs that mimic the intelligent behaviour of people to help them solve problems. This is called artificial intelligence. In this form of computer intelligence, computers, for example, perform well when they are used to make simulated models of new machines such as in car assembly plants. These intelligent robots can be used in industry to perform repetitive tasks, but unlike the human brain they cannot cope with the unexpected or combine perceptions, thoughts and emotions.

A frequent difficulty, however, is that most people even if they get this far, stop here. They don't follow through by assessing the outcome of each small unit's solution and eventually the outcome of the whole problem-solving exercise. It is vital to see whether the problem-solving that you apply to each unit and to the overall stressor, leads to the desired outcome to reduce your stress. If the answer is yes, then can carry on. If the answer is no, you must return to the initial process. And if you exhaust your own efforts at defining and sub-dividing the problem and your own heuristics, you must seek further help elsewhere and appeal to someone else's knowledge and experience.

Once you have resolved that phase of the problem, the next crucial one is to determine (or to assess) how acceptable the solution is to the people who you are going to apply the solution to. You cannot be successful without their and your own feedback. This is vital, because if the solution is acceptable to you, but not to those it is being applied to, you haven't really solved the problem. Someone once said: 'Feedback is the breakfast of champions.' Remember, always aim for a win-win solution.

Sometimes it is necessary for you to explore alternative routes towards problem-solving. Don't always look for a 'cookbook' solution. Life does not consist of a simple set of recipes to follow. Learn how to access information and to obtain enough knowledge about the problem you wish to solve. There is a vast amount of knowledge available for you to use, if only you can find your way to it. Sometimes it is necessary to use methods that are known to solve problems, even if you don't always understand exactly how they work (such as algorithms which consist of a set of rules that you have to follow). Avoid the use of functional fixedness – that is, the tendency to consider only the usual function of an object and to overlook any other possible uses. Be creative in your approach to problem-solving. Remember that creative people tend to be non-conformist, independent, confident, curious and persistent. They use more divergent thinking (that is, they explore novel ideas and side paths) and less convergent thinking (an approach that is aimed at finding a single correct answer). The idea is not to stick to one mental set and to try and solve problems with the same faded, unsuccessful methods.

It is preferable to learn to develop a problem-solving mode of thinking, rather than a problem-creating mode of thinking. This approach is illustrated in Figure 13.1.

CONCLUSION

Goal-directed techniques are necessary, because effective problem-solving can only occur when well-defined steps are pursued. Approaching problem-solving in this way helps you to acknowledge that

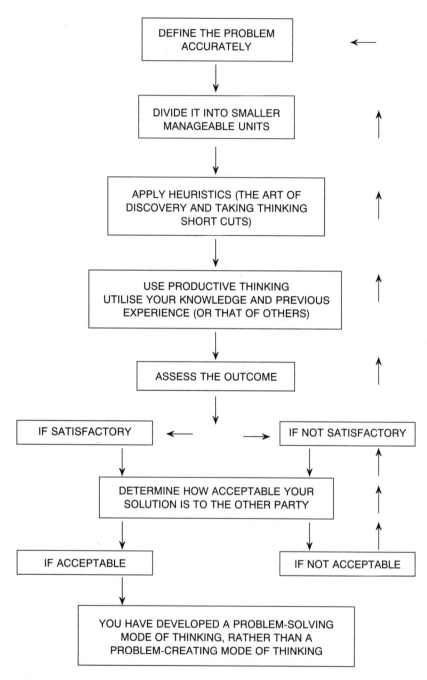

FIGURE 13.1   *A technique for problem-solving.*

the problem exists and to define it accurately. You become aware that you intend to do something about it and gain clarity, understanding and purpose. It also contributes to optimism that problems can be solved if you are prepared to work towards finding an acceptable solution and a willingness to invest energy and skills in it. Good communication and decision-making skills, as well as data collecting, planning and organisational skills are necessary elements in the entire process.

SUMMARY OF THE MAIN PRINCIPLES

- Effective problem-solving skills are essential for stress management.
- Define the problem accurately.
- Divide it into smaller units – not too many and not too complicated because that could also be counter-productive and also cause stress.
- Apply heuristics – the art of discovery/taking thinking short-cuts.
- Use productive thinking – utilise previous experience and knowledge of others.
- Follow through – assess the outcome.
- Assess how acceptable your solution is to the other party – aim for a win-win solution.
- A problem-solving mode of thinking requires the use of goal-directed techniques, good communication and decision-making skills, data collecting, planning and organisational abilities.

CHAPTER 14

Correct your thinking errors

THINKING PROCESSES

IN CHAPTER 7, we discussed the relationship between perception, thoughts, emotions and behaviour. In this chapter we focus more specifically on thoughts and stress. Emotions and feelings start with a core thought. If that core thought causes stressful feelings or emotions, it must be stopped and replaced with one that doesn't. As we have seen, thinking is like self-talk or self-speak – as if you are having an internal dialogue with yourself. The idea then, is to probe your self-speak to determine the thoughts that spark the stress, so that you can identify and correct your thinking errors or distortions. These dysfunctional thoughts that cause you stress are based on mistaken perceptions and develop as a result of past experiences. In a way, they are also associated with faulty thinking patterns that you have acquired through the years. Damaging perceptions were implanted in your thinking long before you could process information rationally, so that over the years an entire thinking pattern evolved that was based on a mistaken beginning. Understanding how this occurs during development will make it clearer.

Research into the development of thinking processes has provided us with some answers. The well-known Swiss biologist, Jean Piaget, proposed an approach to classifying the development of thinking processes in children that is widely accepted. Piaget observed that children understand concepts and reasons differently at different stages. The thinking strategies that a child uses to solve problems reflect an interaction between that particular child's experience in the world and current developmental phase. Birth to age two is the first phase, during which the infant learns through concrete actions by looking, touching, hearing, putting things in the mouth, sucking and grasping. This is the sensory-motor phase, because at this stage the child's 'thinking' consists largely of co-ordinating sensory information with bodily movements. In the second phase (two to seven years of age), thoughts, themes and beliefs are accepted into the child's frontal lobes in the brain. These could either be accurate or based on different logical errors. This is called the pre-operational phase. The third phase is called the concrete operational phase (ages seven to eleven), because the child has difficulty with abstract concepts and thinking is basically on a concrete level. The next phase of formal operations (age 12 to adulthood) marks the beginning of abstract reasoning.

Any misperceptions that occur during phases two and three of intellectual development (that is from two through to eleven years) will be stored in the child's long-term memory and are not easily removed as that child matures. They can lead to dysfunctional thinking patterns. Parents, teachers and friends all have some sort of input into the child developing such thinking patterns. For example, as a child you might have been taught a specific way of thinking which is no longer applicable when you deal with the stress you encounter in your life today. You might, however, be unaware that you are still using the same thinking which, for your current problem, could be totally dysfunctional.

THINKING ERRORS

Such faulty thinking patterns are linked to specific thinking errors which need to be changed to manage stress effectively. The idea is to become aware of such thinking errors so that you can change them to deal with stress more effectively. Once a negative thinking pattern and a specific thinking error have been established, they must be identified and dismantled before you can replace them with positive ones. Some researchers have referred to the process whereby negative thoughts affect you negatively as a form of negative self-speak. The basic technique to change this is 'thought-catching' – catching and changing the thoughts that the negative self-speak cause. Once you have elicited the thought that causes the stress, test it against reality. 'Is it true?' The answer is usually 'No.' If you find that your thoughts act as saboteurs of your reason, and the way you think about your problems interferes with your ability to resolve stress, determine if you use thinking errors in your own negative self-speak. If you do, change them to more functional thoughts. Here are some of the most common thinking errors that people who cope poorly with stress make. Ask yourself whether you use them.

Are you an all-or-nothing thinker? Do you tend to think in absolute terms? An example of this is if you perceive everything in extremes and then have thoughts like: 'I must have the most,' 'I'm nothing but a failure!' or 'Everything always turns out wrong for me!' If you make this kind of thinking error, you set your thinking up to discredit yourself endlessly. Whatever you do, in your mind's eye you will never measure up to your perceptions.

Do you sensationalise? Do you build up ordinary emotions that occur in everyone into dreadful psychological emergencies? Do you think: 'I must have an anxiety disorder because I was nervous before my driver's test?'

Are you a person who tends to over-generalise? Do you tend to expect constant bad luck because of one or two bad or negative experiences?

Do you make temporary little mishaps into permanent ones? Do you think: 'My relationship will never work,' because of one disagreement with your partner?

Do you use a mental filter? Do you screen out all the positives and only concentrate on the negatives? Do you tend to seize a negative fragment from a situation and dwell on it. If you do, it's like wearing a special psychological lens that filters out everything positive in your life and achievements. Your eventual conclusion is that everything is negative, because you focus only on negative parts and then brood on them. That is, you chose specific information to suit dysfunctional thinking which was there in the first place. This creates a vicious cycle of negative thinking and looking for reasons to support it.

Do you always look for the worst possible outcome? Do you think: 'This backache probably means I will never be able to work effectively again'? If you do, you tend to engage in 'awfulising' or worse, 'castrophising'.

Are you an automatic discounter? This occurs when as a product of your dysfunctional thinking, you always brush aside compliments, you discount the good things in life, or the good things in yourself. If someone says to you: 'That's an attractive outfit you're wearing,' do you automatically say to you yourself, 'I wonder what s/he wants.' Do you tend to brush aside compliments by thinking, 'S/he's just being polite.' These thoughts cause poor self-esteem and reinforce your feelings of being a second-rate person.

Do you 'psychologise'? Do you find a psychological reason for everything that happens to you? Don't fall into the trap of 'psychology student's disease' – that is, a believe that you suffer from every psychological symptom you read or hear about. This is common in young psychology students. It can be cured by further study and more knowledge.

Do you jump to conclusions before you have all the facts? Do you make premature (usually incorrect) appraisals?

Do you magnify or minimise problems in order to suit a particular perception or mind set? If you exaggerate or minimise the events that you think about, you worsen the stress. This is sometimes called the 'binocular trick' in which you either blow things up or shrink them out of proportion, including enlarging your own imperfections and decreasing your strengths.

Do you use emotional reasoning or do you reason with the facts? Do you reason with your anger, resentment, guilt, etc. as the most important guide to your thoughts? The emotional reasoner is typical of the person who thinks: 'I must be useless at what I am doing and therefore things never work out for me.' You tend to think badly of yourself because you feel bad. Such thoughts frequently result in more feelings of anger, resentment or guilt and subsequently more stress.

Do you use 'should' statements? Do you live in the past or in the future? Do you tend to say: 'I should have done that' or 'One day I should do this'? Are your thoughts characteristic of someone who reasons: 'I should do this or that to cope better' or 'I should have done this or that to have avoided my stress'? This thinking makes you feel inadequate or guilty rather than motivating you to do something positive about your situation. If you live in the past, or in the future, you permit today to pass you by.

Do you always choose complex explanations, rather than simpler ones?

Do you label, sometimes wrongly, other people or yourself? As we have seen, one of the biggest problems with negative (mis)labelling is that people tend to live up to it, which makes them think they are failures.

Do you always believe something is true, simply because a famous person said so? This is referred to as *ipse dixit*.

Are you always impressed with large numbers? Do you accept that something is true or false simply because many other people think so?

Do you engage in 'permatising'? That is, do you always turn something temporary into a permanent issue? For example: 'I will always be unsuccessful' or 'I will always be anxious.'

Do you use 'musturbation'? That is, do you turn 'wants' into 'musts' or 'shoulds'? For example: 'I must have lots of money to be happy' or 'I should have a new outfit.'

Do you argue ad hominem? That is, do you play the person instead of the ball, such as attacking the individual instead of the individual's argument.

Do you engage in competition? That is, do you always compare yourself to other people and thereby assess your own self-worth in relation to theirs.

Do you use personalisation? Do you tend to take personally things that are never intended to be? If someone makes a comment related to you, do you automatically take it personally, or can you see the wood for the trees? For example, if someone passes an uncomplimentary comment about the colour of your car or its make, do you perceive that as a criticism of you personally? Why should you think the person does not like you because of the colour or make of your car? Personalisation encourages you always to think: 'It's my fault.' You always feel responsible and blame yourself – even for other people's problems or misperceptions. If you do this, you might end up suffering from a sense of 'bogus guilt' and a negative self-concept that will make it difficult for you to cope with stress.

The aim is that once you've changed your perception, you have to identify and change your stress-inducing thinking errors. By replacing thinking errors with positive functional ones, you will find that you move from negative self-speak to positive self-speak. Remember, it has to do with your perceptions and thoughts, which are related. Thoughts produce emotions which result in behaviour. So if you want to change stress-related behaviour, you need to change your negative feelings. To do that, you need to alter your negative, stress-inducing thoughts, and perceive stress through a new psychological 'lens'. Start with the processes in the brain that organise and interpret the stressors in your life – change your perception and then follow it through to those thinking errors.

Think flow not flood. Remember, the weakest link in effective stress management is often the 'weakest think'.

VISUALISE STRESS CONTROL

It's almost like changing a computer program. Now, let's imagine that the program represents your perception and thinking patterns; the typing skills your stress management skills; and the hard copy or printout your stress response. Visualise this in the following way. To effectively use the keyboard of a computer involves typing skills. However, it doesn't matter how skilled you are at typing the keys, the hard copy that your printer will produce will always be faulty or unacceptable if the program in the computer is incorrect. You need not work harder and type faster to achieve the correct printout, but you must change the program if it is faulty or incorrect. Likewise, you will have difficulty in relying entirely on acquired stress management skills discussed in this book to reduce your stress, if you do not change your perception and the faulty thinking patterns that affect your emotions and behaviour which cause the stress. As discussed in Chapter 2, a computer does not hold an opinion on the information it processes, but you do! It can be illustrated as in Figure 14.1.

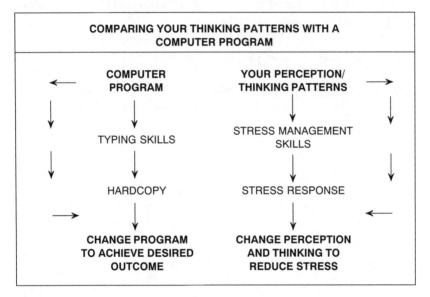

FIGURE 14.1

MONITOR YOUR THOUGHTS

Thoughts that are important in generating and maintaining stress often occur automatically and rapidly, sometimes even beyond your awareness. Sometimes you have to literally tune into them and become aware of any harmful thinking. It is, therefore, useful to keep a daily or weekly record of negative, stress-inducing thoughts so that you can identify them and change them. You also need to note the perceptions, emotional reactions and feelings, as well as the behavioural reactions that these thoughts produce in you, because the influence of your thoughts on them are important to recognise if you want to manage your response to stress. You have to examine the irrationality of some of these thoughts and test how true they are. It is important to determine what effect recurrent negative, stress-inducing thoughts have on your emotions and behaviour and how this causes you stress. A thought record of your stress-inducing thoughts is also a useful way to assess poor tolerance for stress. This technique is based on one of the more effective approaches to teaching people to cope with negative thoughts, and is used in thought-changing therapy. It has become established as an effective psychological tool used as part of a wide range of cognitive behavioural techniques.

The basic technique involves thought-catching and testing negative thoughts against reality as part of problem-solving. To catch these thoughts you literally have to listen to your inner dialogue or self-talk, because by monitoring this you can change your thinking, which will give you more psychological power over your emotions, behaviour and stress response. Recognise all the thoughts that put you down, create self-doubts and regrets and undermine your self-confidence. Don't let them dominate you, but take control so that they can work for you not against you. Your 'thought record' is used to accurately monitor and record your negative thoughts and self-talk whenever they upset you and cause you stress. By recording your thoughts, the link between them and your emotions and behaviour can be clearly demonstrated. It can also be used to test perceptions which give rise to the thoughts that cause you stress. This helps you to see if these thoughts are in fact correct. Such reality-testing aims to seek evidence for and against your negative thoughts and assumptions. One of the big problems with negative thoughts is that they always seem so indisputable to you. But writing them down makes them less intimidating, because then they seem more like thoughts to you and less like reality. It is also easier then for you to generate alternative solutions to the problem that causes them.

You might find that negative thoughts often produce stress because they activate long-held fears. By recalling how these fears started and how you have kept them going (usually unnecessarily or irrationally), you can learn to set them aside. Remember that your stress reactions are often based on perception and interpretation rather than on fact. If this causes negative thoughts and stress, you should aim to replace them with believable, more rational ones. That is, switch from dysfunctional, stress-inducing thoughts to functional, stress-reducing thoughts. Look again at Table 7.1 where you were shown how alternative perceptions or interpretations can reduce stress. In exactly the same way, you can change negative thoughts to positive ones and remove any emotional roadblocks in this process that cause wrong attributions or blame for your stress. Let bygones be bygones and stop carrying the emotional baggage of the past. Your stress-inducing thought record could look something like the one illustrated in Table 14.1.

INTERNAL DIALOGUE

You can change your internal dialogue positively if you replace negative with positive thoughts and correct any thinking errors you might harbour. By becoming aware of your self-speak (internal dialogue) you can identify negative, self-defeating thoughts that cause stress and change them to more positive, self-enhancing, less stressful ones. By doing so, any feelings of helplessness and hopelessness can be shifted to feelings of strength and hopefulness. Your inner language often reflects how you feel about yourself. To make this more positive, replace phrases such as: 'I can't' with 'I prefer not to' or 'I haven't learnt to'; 'always' with 'sometimes' or 'at this time'; 'I should' to 'I choose'; 'I never' to 'I seldom' or 'I rarely'; 'I can't get any further' to 'I'm pausing to explore other options'; 'I have to' to 'I want to' or 'I will', etc. Practise changing negative self-statements to positive ones, and avoid rehearsing negative experiences in your mind. Rather rehearse correcting it and then visualise the successful outcome. This is also sometimes called reframing. Never forget that positive self-statements and phrases lead to positive results and less stress.

For example, depressed people use a thinking (cognitive) strategy that focuses on what is wrong, rather than what is right. Typically their depressive thoughts can be classified in terms of a cognitive triad, as originally postulated by A. Beck who is well known for his work on depression: A negative view of the self ('I am a failure'), the world ('This is a dreadful place'), and the future ('My future is hopeless'). In addition, such people make thinking errors, have negative automatic thoughts (that is, depressing thoughts that come out of the blue), and depressogenic schemas (that is, long-lasting attitudes and assumptions by which they persistently classify information about the world in a negative way).

On the other hand, people who suffer from anxiety use a cognitive strategy that focuses on 'what ifs'. They fill their minds with a welter of frightening fears that cause unnecessary stress – all based on an 'If this', 'If that', 'What if I', 'What if the lift gets stuck', 'What if this pain is a dreadful disease', etc. Typically they have a unique combination of unpleasant thoughts and physiological changes related to the activation of the autonomic nervous system. This produces apprehension, tension and nervousness which can sometimes be so overwhelming that it can cause panic attacks. This is discussed in more detail in Chapters 2 and 5.

Such negative cognitive strategies should be recognised and the necessary shifts in your internal dialogue to a more positive focus should be made. You can do this by re-arranging your thinking patterns as discussed in this chapter. It will bring more lasting changes in stress reduction because your self-speak can create a desirable self-image and enhanced confidence to deal with stress.

MIND-RACING

An area that often causes stress is when your thoughts start to accelerate, so that you end up experiencing what is commonly referred to as mind-racing. Your thoughts are usually based on thinking errors that race around in circles. You keep on trying to rethink the past or the future, considering numerous alternatives. This often occurs at night, but not necessarily so. You can stop these accelerated thought processes and thinking errors by practising a few basic techniques:

- Identify the cause. This is often rooted in the wrong definition of the problem or in too many choices (some even opposing ones) as a result of frustration and conflict.
- Apply your psychological brake and use the memory aid A WASP to reduce the stress caused by your racing thoughts (see Chapter 8).
- Apply the problem-solving technique discussed earlier.
- Eliminate thinking errors.
- If you identify negative emotions as a result of the racing thoughts, deal with the emotion.
- But, make sure that you deal with the right emotion.
- Deal with any muscular or physical tension that arises from the mind-racing.
- If you have learnt a basic relaxation exercise, practise it.
- This will also help you to calm your thoughts and divert them.
- As your body relaxes and you regain psychological control, your mind will relax.
- If you find that most of your mind-racing occurs at night, avoid taking any substances that mimic the stress response well before you retire. The main ones were discussed in Chapter 5 when we looked at the whole problem of stress and substance abuse.

TABLE 14.1

		THOUGHT-MONITORING RECORD		
DATE	STRESSOR	THOUGHTS	EMOTIONS	BEHAVIOUR
	Describe the actual stressors that lead to the thoughts, emotions and behaviour.	Describe your stress-inducing thoughts.	Describe how the thoughts make you feel. Specify the emotions that upset you.	Describe what the thoughts and emotions make you want to do.
?	**Example 1** A pedestrian steps in front of my car and I nearly run the person over.	**Negative** What a stupid fool! Why can't people be more careful? = emotional reasoning. **Switch to alternative positive** It pays to be alert when driving. I am glad that it wasn't an accident.	**Negative** Extreme anger, hostility. **Positive** Relief, self-worth, dignity.	**Negative** Slam on brakes, unwind the window and scream at the pedestrian. Stress. **Positive** Controlled temper. Proceed with caution. Situation under control. Less stress.
?	**Example 2** At a critical moment my computer would not respond the way I wanted it to.	**Negative** Nothing I do ever comes out right = over-generalising depressogenic thinking. **Switch to alternative positive** Many things I do often come out right.	**Negative** Depression, low self-worth, self-pity, hopelessness. **Positive** Hopefulness, confidence, enthusiasm, optimistic.	**Negative** Wanting to give up, poor work performance, disinterest. Stress. **Positive** Trying harder, better work performance, enhanced interest, motivated. Less stress.

CONCLUSION

Never forget that the thinking errors which lead to stressful emotional and behavioural reactions don't always depend on the external reality of your stressors, but on your perception and interpretation. So, to reduce stress, you have to change the way you process information and go beyond the immediate perception of the stressors. You have to remove bias in your information processing. By doing this, you will soon learn that correcting your thinking errors can go a long way to intervene between your perceived stress and your actual stress response. Because the perceived meaning or significance of the stress will affect the degree of stress you experience, you often react to what your perception prompts you to think about the stressor rather than to the stressor itself – that is, rather than to the actual stimulus that produces the stress. This wrong perception also activates thinking errors. For example, the person who panics in a crowded traffic situation might base this on the perception that he or she will lose control. This triggers off a thinking error. The resultant stress reaction can then be disproportionate to what is reasonable – 'larger than life'. Another example is, if you experience a stress reaction simply because you park your new car in a crowded open parking lot with free parking, you are clearly reacting to more than just owning and parking a new car. For example, you might be entertaining various thinking errors like what if it gets scratched when I'm away? I'm still paying it off! Maybe I should have parked in the covered paid section. These thoughts only serve to increase your stress.

So, you should start by finding the perceptions linked to those thoughts that cause negative emotions and behaviours and produce stress. These should then be analysed in an effort to assess their validity and usefulness. In this way you can determine whether a particular perception is in fact a misinterpretation and a particular thought is irrational, negative and stress-producing – that is, a thinking error. The idea is to shift from those thoughts that are unrealistic and harmful to those that are realistic, rational and useful. Many people suffer from stress-producing thoughts, and often they suffer in silence. You don't have to be one of them.

SUMMARY OF THE MAIN PRINCIPLES

- Identify and correct your thinking errors.
- They are based on mistaken perceptions and develop as a result of past experiences.
- It's almost like changing a computer program.
- The basic technique involves thought-catching and testing negative thoughts against truth and reality.
- It also involves making a perceptual shift.
- Keep a stress monitoring thought record to help you.

CHAPTER 15

Develop a wellness programme

PSYCHOLOGICAL HEALTH

THE worth of a thing is what it will bring. Being psychologically well implies maturity, competence, a balance in psychic forces, the full realisation of one's potential and a perception that does not result in a distortion of reality. It embraces feeling successful in working, loving, creating and the capacity for mature and flexible resolution of conflicts and stress, as well as resistance to negative stress. Health and well-being are two of the most precious things you could ever have. They can help you unlock your true potential.

Psychological health is not freedom from stress but involves a balanced lifestyle, which includes an overall balanced relationship with your world. In fact, as emphasised in Chapter 4, the World Health Organisation defines health as a complete state of physical, psychological and social well-being. Put differently, the absence of disease is not necessarily a sign of health. The fact that you are not feeling sick right now doesn't automatically mean that you are healthy. The fact that your body and mind do not show the effects of negative stress right now, doesn't mean that they are not lurking somewhere inside.

There are many ways of coping with stress, as discussed in this book. Many others are also reliable, but some are rather dubious or have potential risks. Make sure you choose the right ones. One of the most effective and enduring strategies to cope with stress is to develop a personal wellness programme and healing image which incorporates what I've said before. This implies making the necessary changes in your lifestyle. My own experience has taught me that changing your perception is a crucial component in making lifestyle changes if you want to deal effectively with stress and take charge of yourself. This involves a whole new thinking process. We have seen that your responses are not just the reaction of emotions. They are also reactions because of your perceptions and thoughts. If you change these you can feel and respond in the way you choose to. You are free to make this choice. But it also means undoing the knots of your past and freeing yourself from old psychological ropes that, although maybe somewhat frayed by now, still prevent you from developing psychological wellness in the present. Don't let the past hold you back. Let it go – it's finished. You can't change it. But you can change your 'now'. Don't lose the experience of 'now' so that it becomes yet another bit of past to worry about. Your power lies in the present, because this is where you can make changes.

Emotions and stress are discussed in more detail in Chapter 7. Some of the most futile emotions that prevent you from dealing with stress are the negative ones. They arise from your negative perceptions and thoughts. They include guilt, worry, anger and fear. Guilt paralyses your present efforts to deal with stress because it traps you in your past behaviour. Worry immobilises your current efforts to deal with stress because it traps you in the future. In the same vein, one of the most outstanding features of psychologically healthy people is that they do not to let their anger hamper their ability to deal with stress. Like all emotions, anger is the result of your perceptions and thoughts – which makes it a choice that lets you behave in ways that produce few, if any, psychological rewards for you. We saw in Chapter 11 that assertiveness is a necessary element of good stress management and that bottling up anger is not desirable. This does not mean you should not feel angry at times, but you must find more constructive ways of channelling your anger if it does arise. Inappropriately expressing anger does not always get rid of anger – sometimes it prolongs it because you rehearse being upset, unnecessarily pump up your blood pressure and create a poor psychological climate. Controlling your temper makes you feel calmer, less angry and less stressed. So, do not allow anger to debilitate your psychological wellness and stress-management skills. Say farewell to it as a choice in dealing with stress. Don't waste your time and energy on anger as a solution. Rather explore the causes of your anger and solve them.

Like anger, fear can prevent you from making the most of the present. Moderate amounts of fear can be a protection, but excessive fear can be paralysing. It causes resistance to change and further procrastination. Some people actually fear living life. This keeps them on the go in such a way that they never really face themselves, or realise their potential. They want to be stress free, feel more and be happier, but are afraid of life. People who are afraid of not opening up and reaching out to others, isolate themselves because of their fear of rejection. This ironically ensures that they are rejected. You are not free if you erect massive psychological walls as a protection against possible stress. What you are likely to discover is that the stress you fear is often locked up in this very process. So, do not allow yourself to be a victim of guilt, worry, anger and fear. Don't let these emotions stop you from changing and experiencing the present.

A WELLNESS PROGRAMME

Develop a wellness programme and a healing image. Practise the suggestions listed: they will enable you to prevent or cope better with the disabling effects of stress. Some of the techniques listed involve easy ones, such as exercise, relaxation techniques, taking diet supplements, regular holidays or breaks, or deliberately slowing down your pace of life. Others are more involved and require more effort, but are nevertheless attainable – especially if you take the initiative and sustain your efforts.

- Accept that change and stress are part of life and that stress can be a paradox – you need it in the right amounts.
- Understand what stress is all about.
- Learn the value of exposure to positive stress. Remember that not all stress is bad for you. Some stress is actually necessary and even quite good. You need a certain state of activation or arousal to perform optimally. When the stress becomes difficult to cope with, disproportionate and prolonged, then it becomes a problem.
- Learn to recognise your mind and body's response to stress. In this process, you need to be proactive. Don't wait for the disease or the discomfort to hit you. Prevent it. Assess your own personal stress levels.
- Identify the causes of your stress and your life pressures, both long-term life events and daily hassles. Very often those small daily hassles that you overlook are the silent major stressors.
- If you do have a problem with stress, admit it. It is nothing to be ashamed of. Admit that to cope, you have to do something – that the solution lies within yourself. Just being aware of how stressed you are and that you can do something about it, are important steps in the right direction.
- Stress is often the result of your perception. That is, it is in the 'eye of the beholder'. Sometimes it exists only in the mind. So change your perception of your stressor. Use your mind as a tool that can work for you – not against you. Re-evaluate the situation by looking at it from a different perspective. Screen out the negative thoughts once you have identified them. Then replace them with positive thoughts.
- Don't allow yourself to be flooded by events. Learn to flow with them. Don't be inflexible to change.

- Try to adopt an optimistic and enthusiastic life approach. Those who are optimistic are better able to cope with stress and less apt to suffer from a stress-related disorder, and if they should develop such a disorder they tend to recover more easily. Laugh a little. A daily dose of humour is a great technique for combatting stress.
- Identify keyed-up feelings that your lifestyle might produce, and then manage your lifestyle by changing what is required. Aim for a balance between the cornerstones of what life is really all about. Some examples are family, work and leisure. Try to work out a balance between these aspects of your life. Balance your left- and right-brain activities.
- Avoid living and working in a clutter by making the necessary changes.
- Learn effective stress management through self-management and effective time management. Deal with work stress timeously.
- Improve your relationships and learn to be comfortable with the success of other people. Don't let their success cause you stress because of your own unresolved needs.
- Develop appropriate people skills. Develop effective communication, listening and speaking skills and learn to manage conflict successfully. Improve your negotiating skills and always seek win-win solutions.
- Be more assertive, less aggressive and less submissive and develop a positive self-image.
- Develop a pleasing personality.
- Develop a problem-solving mode of thinking, not a problem-creating mode of thinking.
- Recognise thinking errors that you make and change them.
- Use imagery as a tool to help you cope. Imagery involves the inner representation of objects and events that you create in your mind. Images are used in many areas of thought changing. Select specific images to help you change wrong perceptions and thinking errors. Because images do not involve language, they are extremely useful in making these changes. Examples of images include: coping images (imagine yourself being able to cope with stress); relaxing images (imagine relaxing, pleasant surroundings); rewarding images (imagine the reward you will reap if you manage your stress); mastery images (imagine coping successfully with your work and with your personal relationships), etc. Use the simple technique of imagining your mind to be an empty television screen. You can put whatever you want on that screen. It is your choice which channel you want to tune

into. You can visualise where you want to be, or what you want to do, and then you can act and perform optimally according to those visualisations.

- Be less self-centred. Take an interest in something bigger than yourself.
- Remember what you put into life you get back. The old adage 'what you sow, you will reap' is never truer than in stress management.
- Explore your own personality. Get to know yourself. Change the harmful aspects of the Type A personality if they apply to you. It is particularly the time-urgent, aggressive and hostility components of the Type A personality that have to be modified to avoid adverse health consequences.
- Seek help for psychological disorders if you should suffer from them.
- Use correct breathing techniques. Problems in breathing are one of the best indicators of stress, as it reflects many of your adjustment functions and your general state of stress arousal. Such problems may have emotional or physical causes. If you want to test whether you breathe correctly, a simple procedure is to put one hand on your chest and one on your stomach and then to feel how you breathe while you are in a rested state. The bottom hand (the hand on your stomach) should move out when you inhale and the top hand (the hand on your chest) should be virtually still. The aim is to achieve correct breathing and relaxation by abdominal/ diaphragmatic breathing. If both hands move as you breathe, you are chest breathing. On the other hand, if your abdomen moves in and your chest expands when you inhale, you are reverse breathing. If you breathe more than 14 breaths per minute, the chances are you are breathing too rapidly for someone who is in a rested state. If you do correct breathing exercises, you can go a long way in dealing with stress. Ideally you should breathe through the nose, because it prepares the air for the lungs. Although breathing is an involuntary, automatic function it can be controlled and correct breathing can be learnt. Correct breathing promotes relaxation and controls tension and stress. As with laughing, deep breathing allows the effective intake of air. It also helps to strengthen and condition the pulmonary system and the cardiovascular system, promote oxygenation and it plays an important role in the prevention and treatment of certain psychosomatic and stress-related problems, and generally promotes restfulness.
- Exercise regularly. Stay fit for life not only psychologically, but also physically. Why is exercise so important, apart from all the well-

known good and positive spin offs? Not only does it take care of the 'fight-or-flight' response when you are in a state of arousal because of stress, but in today's consumer-hungry world, we tend to settle too easily into the 'good life'. The negative consequences of this together with an inactive lifestyle compound the harmful effects. Consequently, many people become unnaturally depressed, anxious or stressed and ultimately develop other stress-related disorders – which are some of the most common disorders that affect society today. Exercise therapy has been shown to be a very effective treatment for many stress-related problems. For example, it has been demonstrated that healthy adults who exercise regularly tend to score lower on stress tests after engaging in an exercise programme, and many investigations have supported the evidence that exercise therapy can assist in the treatment of depression. So, it is not unreasonable to talk of the anti-stress or anti-depressant effects of appropriate exercise. Also, we tend to be less likely to think about unpleasant things while we exercise, so that exercise provides the additional bonus of a built-in aid to correcting those thinking errors that are so necessary for stress reduction.

- Physical and mental relaxation are important stress-reducers. There are many relaxation programmes available ranging from physical ones such as progressive muscle relaxation, to mental ones such as meditation. The more you practise these, the more they become part of your everyday lifestyle.
- Strive for inner peace. You have to feed not only your body, but also your soul.
- Practice mental diversion. A good way to do that is to get a non-competitive hobby. Remember the benefits you derive from mental diversion, sleep, physical exercise, mental exercise or meditation are all different.
- Vent steam. Don't bottle up your feelings. Don't walk around with unspent emotions. Talk or write about them. The age-old belief that confession is good for body and soul has a sound basis. Sometimes perceiving and thinking of an event as stressful causes stress, but trying to change your perception or to stop thinking about it can also be stressful. However, failure to confront an issue forces you to live with it in an unresolved manner. Actively talking or writing about it can give you insight and provide some emotional distance as well as relief – not only because you are venting your feelings but also because you are sharing them with someone, even if that someone is imaginary.

- Get enough sleep. Your brain and your body needs rest to deal with stress.
- Remember, in many ways you are what you eat. I often advise people not to 'dig their grave with their teeth'. Stress affects your body at all levels. Stress robs you of vitality and wellness through depletion of the necessary nutrients. Many people are unaware that nutrition can play a significant role in emotional stability and handling stress. Maintain a proper diet. Eat well not only for physical health, but also for mental health. Recognise the value of good nutrition and especially of vitamins, minerals and trace elements in stress management. And if your diet is not sufficient or if you are unwell, or if you are experiencing very high stress levels, you can always supplement your diet with appropriate choices. Think of it like this: 'The more junk food, the more junk behaviour, the more general nutritional deficiencies, the more difficult it is to deal with stress.
- Use constructive self-talk. Give yourself a daily pep talk. Become your own best friend.
- Change harmful attitudes and beliefs and get rid of your prejudices. Shed that extra emotional load they cause. Let go of the psychological burdens of the past and the extra emotional baggage you carry along with it. You don't carry unnecessary physical loads, so why carry unnecessary emotional loads?
- Deal with specific negative emotions, should you harbour them towards another. A useful technique to deal with the feelings they cause is to wish that person well. Why allow a person whom you think has caused problems for you to continue harming you psychologically?
- You should help and support your fellow humans, but guard against always playing the 'rescuer' or 'hero' role as it will only increase your own stress. If you always give care, but never receive care, you are at risk of increased stress levels.
- Learn to forgive.
- Learn to take criticism positively.
- Develop the ability to recover quickly. Visualise yourself as a rubber ball that doesn't stay down, but bounces back. How many times you stumble or fall is unimportant – what matters is how many times you get back up.
- Watch your body language and that of others. Non-verbal aspects of behaviour, such as appropriate eye contact, smiling, observing, listening, etc. are important in stress management.
- Seek social support, seek family support, seek support at work.

- Aim for a healthy work and home environment.
- Seek spiritual nourishment.
- Try to improve your memory. There are many different techniques that you can learn.
- Learn to cope with special needs. For example, many modern families have special needs such as dual career families, single parent families, etc.
- Do not over-stretch your finances. Successful financial planning in our modern world is a prerequisite for reducing stress caused by financial problems and other demands. It will also assist you to have more money to pursue your relaxation activities and have more fun.
- Think yourself healthier. Aim to transform failure into success.
- Keep a regular well-being diary. This will help you to acknowledge and tap into any stressful thoughts and feelings. Frequently simply acknowledging negative thoughts and emotions is enough to reduce stress.
- Discover your own potential through aiming for realistic expectations.
- Put meaning into your life. People constantly seek answers to questions like: 'What's it all about?' 'What's the point?' Because humans are so different, you need to find meaning and what is fulfilling and self-actualising for you.
- Develop your own personal mission statement. Visualise yourself sometime into the future. What would you like to have achieved? Now try to live according to that mission statement.
- Ultimately aim for psychological self-empowerment, so that you don't feel like a victim of stress.

CONCLUSION

It is up to you. Remind yourself always that it starts with you. There are times when you have to believe in yourself. When you know there is nobody else. At such times you know you are ready to become a person of wisdom. If you want to deal with the negative stress in your life, don't delay – start now! Reading this book is the first step in a process – a lifelong process. Put an end to further procrastination. There is no time like the present. Start changing now. I have given you some pointers on how to do this. The rest is up to you! Think like a winner!

SUMMARY OF THE MAIN PRINCIPLES

- Develop a lifestyle that incorporates a wellness programme and healing image.
- Psychological health is not freedom from stress, but an overall balanced lifestyle.
- This means making necessary lifestyle changes.

References

American Psychiatric Association (APA). *Diagnostic and Statistical Manual of Mental Disorders.* DSM-IV. Fourth Edition. Washington DC: American Psychiatric Association, 1994.

Behavioral Science Task Force of the National Advisory Mental Health Council. Basic Behavioral Science Research for Mental Health: A National Investment: Emotion and Motivation. *American Psychologist*, 50, pp 838–845, 1995.

Berglas, S. *The Success Syndrome: Hitting Bottom when you Reach the Top.* New York: Plenum, 1986.

Blanton, B. *Radical Honesty: How to Transform your Life by Telling the Truth.* New York: Dell Publishing, 1996.

Bolton, R. *People Skills: How to Assert Yourself, Listen to Others and Resolve Conflicts.* New York: Simon & Schuster, 1979.

Chaitow, L. *The Stress Protection Plan: How to Stay Healthy Under Pressure.* London: Thorsons, 1992.

Corney, R. *Developing Communication and Counselling Skills in Medicine.* London: Tavistock/ Routledge, 1991.

Costa, P.T. and Van den Bos, G.R. (Eds). *Psychological Aspects of Serious Illness: Chronic Conditions, Fatal Diseases, and Clinical Care.* Washington DC: American Psychological Association, 1990.

Feuerstein, M., Labbé, E.E. and Kuczmierczyk, A.R. *Health Psychology: A Psychobiological Perspective.* New York: Plenum, 1986.

Freedy, J.R. and Hobfoll, S.E. *Traumatic Stress: From Theory to Practice.* New York: Plenum, 1995.

Fried, R. *The Breath Connection: How to Reduce Psychosomatic and Stress-Related Disorders with Easy-to-do Breathing Exercises.* New York: Plenum, 1990.

Friedman, H.S. (Ed.). *Personality and Disease.* New York: Wiley, 1990.

Goleman, D. *Emotional Intelligence: Why it can Matter more than IQ.* New York: Bantam Books, 1995.

Hayes, N. *Foundations of Psychology: An Introductory Text.* London: Routledge, 1994.

Hodgkinson, P.E. and Stewart, M. *Coping with Catastrophe: A Handbook of Post-Disaster Psychosocial Aftercare.* London: Routledge, 1998.

Hogan, R., Curphy, G.J. and Hogan, J. 'What we Know about Leadership, Effectiveness and Personality'. *American Psychologist*, 49, pp 493–504, 1994.

Izard, C.E. *The Psychology of Emotions.* New York: Plenum, 1991.

Johnsgård, K.W. *The Exercise Prescription for Depression and Anxiety.* New York: Plenum, 1989.

Kaplan, H.J., Sadock, B.J. and Grebb, J.A. (Eds). *Kaplan and Sadock's Synopsis of Psychiatry. Behavioural Sciences/Clinical Psychiatry.* Seventh Edition. Maryland: Williams and Wilkins, 1994.

Kleber, R.J., Figley, C.R. and Gersons, B.P.R. *Beyond Trauma: Cultural and Societal Dynamics.* New York: Plenum, 1995.

Koslowsky, M., Kluger, A.N. and Reich M. *Commuting Stress: Causes, Effects, and Methods of Coping.* New York: Plenum, 1995.

Markham, U. *Managing Stress: The Practical Guide to Using Stress Positively.* Shaftesbury: Element Books, 1989.

Marsella, A.J., Friedman, M.J., Gerrity, E.T. and Scurfield, R.M. *Ethnocultural Aspects of Posttraumatic Stress Disorder: Issues, Research, and Clinical Applications.* Washington DC: American Psychological Association, 1996.

Martorano, J.T. and Kildahl, J.P. *Beyond Negative Thinking: Breaking the Cycle of Depressing and Anxious Thoughts.* New York: Plenum, 1989.

Masters, W.H. and Johnson, V.E. *Human Sexual Response.* Boston: Little Brown & Co, 1966.

Masters, W.H., Johnson, V.E. and Kolodny, R.C. *Human Sexuality.* Fourth Edition. New York: Harper Collins, 1992.

Mc Mullin, R.E. *Handbook of Cognitive Therapy Techniques.* New York: W.W. Norton, 1986.

Mkhondo, R. 'Faith and Medicine: Placebo or Higher Power? Doctors make faith part of the cure'. *Daily News*, 18 December 1997.

Morgan, B. and Morgan, R. *Brain Food.* London: Michael Joseph, 1986.

Nierenberg, G. and Calero, H. *How to Read a Person Like a Book.* London: Thorsons, 1973.

Pease, A. *Body Language: How to Read Others' Thoughts by their Gestures.* Avalon Beach NSW, Australia: Camel, 1992.

Pennebaker, J.W. (Ed.). *Emotion, Disclosure & Health.* Washington DC: American Psychological Association, 1995.

Rice, P.L. *Stress & Health.* Second Edition. Pacific Grove, California: Brooks/Cole, 1992.

Schlebusch, L. *Conduct Disorders in Youth.* Durban: Butterworths, 1979.

Schlebusch, L. (Ed.). *Clinical Health Psychology: A Behavioural Medicine Perspective.* Halfway House: Southern Book Publishers, 1990.

Schlebusch, L. (Ed.). *Depression: A Basic Guide to Diagnosis and Treatment.* Johannesburg: Ciba-Geigy, 1990.

Schlebusch, L. (Ed.). *Cancer Can Be Beaten: A Biopsychosocial Approach.* Durban: Sub-Department of Medically Applied Psychology, University of Natal, 1993.

Schlebusch, L. (Ed.). *Suicidal Behaviour 3.* Proceedings of the Third Southern African Conference on Suicidology. Durban: Sub-Department of Medically Applied Psychology, University of Natal, 1995.

Schlebusch, L. Health Psychology in South Africa: An Introduction. *South African Journal of Psychology*, 20, 1–3, 1996.

Schlebusch, L. (Ed.). *South Africa Beyond Transition: Psychological Well-being.* Pretoria: Psychological Society of South Africa, 1998.

Schlebusch, L. *Proverbial Stress Busters.* Cape Town: Human & Rousseau, 1998.

Schlebusch, L. *Psychological Recovery from Cancer*. Johannesburg: Maskew Miller Longman, 1999.

'Scientists stay on the side of the angels'. *New York Times*, as reported in the *Natal Mercury*, 4 April 1997, p. 7.

Scott, M. *A Cognitive-Behavioural Approach to Clients' Problems*. London: Tavistock/Routledge, 1989.

Shadwell, A., Schlebusch, L. and Van Niekerk, W.C.A. Stress and the Sick Building Syndrome. Biopsychosocial Health-Related Variables Affecting Workers Employed in South African Urban Places where Live Discotheque Music Entertainment is Provided. In: Smith, A. (Ed.), *2000 Then What?* 13th International Clean Air & Environment Conference. Adelaide: The Clean Air Society of Australia and New Zealand Inc., pp 621–633, 1996.

Shadwell, A., Schlebusch, L. and Van Niekerk, W.C.A. Stress and the Sick Building Syndrome in Places where Live or Discotheque Musical Entertainment is Provided. In: S. Yoshizawa, et al. (Eds). *Indoor Air '96*. Proceedings of the International Conference on Indoor Air Quality and Climate, Volume 4. Tokyo, pp 249–254, 1996.

Sleek, S. Isolation increases with Internet use. *APA Monitor*, 1 and 30–31, September 1998.

Solomon, E.P., Schmidt, R.R. and Adragna, P.J. *Human Anatomy & Physiology*. Second Edition. Orlando, Florida: Saunders College Publishing, 1990.

Sternberg, R.J. *In Search of the Human Mind*. Orlando, Florida: Harcourt Brace, 1995.

Stroebe, W. and Stroebe M.S. *Bereavement and Health: The Psychological and Physical Consequences of Partner Loss*. New York: Cambridge University, 1987.

Strydom, L. (Ed.). *Management Communications Handbook*. Pretoria: MIMS, 1991.

Temoshok, L. and Dreher, H. *Recognizing and Changing Type C Behaviour*. In: ten Have-de Labije, J. and Balner, H. (Eds). *Coping with Cancer and Beyond: Cancer Treatment & Mental Health*. Amsterdam/Lisse: Swets and Zeitlinger, pp 80–98, 1991.

Van der Kolk, B.A., McFarlane, A.C. and Weissaath, L. (Eds). *Traumatic Stress: The Effects of Overwhelming Experience on Mind, Body and Society*. New York: Guildford Press, 1996.

Varma, V.P. *Stress in Psychotherapists*. London: Routledge, 1997.

Wade, C. and Tavris, C. *Psychology*. New York: Harper & Row, 1990.

Warren, E. and Toll, C. *The Stress Work Book: How Individuals, Teams and Organisations can Balance Pressure and Performance*. London: Nicholas Brealey, 1993.

Williams, J.M.G. *The Psychological Treatment of Depression: A Guide to the Theory and Practice of Cognitive Behaviour Therapy*. Second Edition. London: Routledge, 1984.

Index